FELLED OAKS

Other books by André Malraux:

Anti-Memoirs
The Metamorphosis of the Gods
The Voices of Silence
Saturn, an Essay on Goya
Man's Hope
Man's Fate
The Royal Way
The Conquerors
The Temptation of the West

‡

FELLED OAKS

Conversation with De Gaulle

by
André Malraux

Holt, Rinehart and Winston
New York
Chicago
San Francisco

Published simultaneously in Canada by Holt, Rinehart and Winston of Canada, Limited.

ISBN: 0–03–091166–4
Library of Congress Catalog Card Number: 72–182758
Originally published in French under the title of Les Chênes qu'on abat. . . .

First published in the United States in 1972

Translated from the French by Irene Clephane, revised by Linda Asher

Printed in the United States of America

Portions of this book appeared in Esquire *Magazine.*

Photograph on page 11 by Giséle Freund/Photo Researchers

Ah, what a dreadful sound they make in the waning light,
The oaks being felled for Hercules' pyre!

Victor Hugo

PREFACE

My reasons for publishing now these fragments from the second volume of *Antimémoires* will be clear to anyone who reads them.

Also, in correcting these proofs, I found that they formed a book. The act of creation has always interested me more than perfection, a preference which led to constant disagreement between me and André Gide, and to my admiration, from the time I was twenty years old, for Braque and for Picasso. This book is an interview in the same way that *La Condition humaine* was a report: that is to say, not at all.

I have discovered, with surprise, that we possess no dialogue between a man of history and a great artist, whether painter, writer, or musician. All we know of Julius II's conversations with Michelangelo is their wrangling; nor of Alexander's with the philosophers, Augustus's with the poets, Tamerlane's with Ibn Khaldoun. It is astonishing that Voltaire left no record of his conversations with Frederick. Diderot talked brilliantly to Sophie Volland about his evenings at the Castle of Holbach, but never recorded his conversations with Catherine the Great. Napoleon soliloquizes even on Saint Helena. He may have received Goethe splendidly, but it was "in audience." Victor Hugo reconstructs for us his conversations with Louis Philippe, but what does Louis Philippe matter? Chateaubriand recounts his conversations at Prague, with the exiled Charles X asking him insignificant questions while the royal children of France climbed on his knees begging, "Monsieur de Chateaubriand, tell us the story of the Holy Sepulcher!" Why did he not go to Saint Helena rather than to Prague? From such a visit might have sprung his finest chapter: "Before this tumbledown cottage, so like my own, a man wearing a planter's hat was waiting for me. I scarcely recognized Bonaparte. We went indoors, we lost ourselves in the fate of the world; and while he talked low of Austerlitz, the eagles of Saint Helena wheeled across the windows open on eternity. . . ."

Even when the man of history has witnesses, he does not discourse with them (Napoleon with Roederer, Saint Louis with Joinville). For no shorthand has caught a conversation, or even an improvised speech. Jaurès never allowed his talks to be published until he had written them after the event. If only by our odd spoken syntax ("Well, so then his sister, she said . . . ,"), television demonstrates clearly the difference between the written word and the disorder of the spoken word (except for the reading of a text). Voltaire might have recreated his conversations with Frederick; Thierry d'Argenlieu would not his with General de Gaulle. In the past, for an interview to take place would have required that its reporting be regarded as significant; that it be a conversation, not an audience; and that he who reported it be capable of recreating it. And this brings us to our century.

But we must not take outbursts for confidences. It would be fascinating for us if we could "listen in" on a conversation of this kind with Napoleon because it would be fascinating to learn what Napoleon used to say *freely*. Marshal Bertrand often gives us some idea of this, but here too Napoleon speaks almost solo; and Bertrand was no writer. What General de Gaulle says in this book portrays him, sometimes in a fairly private domain. But his remarks range from topics on which he had already reflected (the opening exposition, as always with him—or sentences which he had said or written before), to some impromptu ideas set out for further consideration, then on to things said for amusement—and even to the underlying vein of things it did not suit him to discuss.

I have tried to show a General de Gaulle within history and outside history, and hence the presence here of insignificant passages. Why not omit them? To do so would change the color of the meeting, and the tone of the *Antimémoires* (in which this meeting will recur) would be destroyed. I did not want a photographic portrait; I dreamed of producing an El Greco, but not an El Greco drawn from an imaginary model. When I was writing these pages, I intended them for posthumous publication. My purpose was to set down not a dialogue between General de Gaulle and myself, but a dialogue between a will that held France at arm's length, and the snow which covered the vast forests, empty of villages since the Great Invasions, and which the General was wearily folding about him. It all came to an end with my departure from Colombey and nightfall. Fate took care of the epilogue.

Ten minutes after his death, the doctor left La Boisserie to go and treat a railwayman's daughters. Madame de Gaulle asked one of the coffinmakers to take the wedding ring from the General's finger; their work scarcely done, the two workmen were summoned by Madame Plique whose husband, a farmer, had just died . . . as well. Two days later, in the gray day of the funeral ceremonies, I hurried along under the tolling bell of Colombey, echoed by all the belfries in

France, and in my memory by all the bells of the Liberation. I saw the open tomb, the two enormous wreaths lying beside it, from Mao Tse-tung and Chou En-lai. In Peking, the flags flew at half-mast over the Forbidden City. At Colombey, in the little church without a past, there would be the parish, the family, the Order:* a knight's interment. The radio was telling us that in Paris, on the Champs Élysées he walked down long ago, a silent multitude climbed, carrying to the Arc de Triomphe daisies dripping with rain—a tribute France had not offered since the death of Victor Hugo.

Here at Colombey, in the crowd behind the marines presenting arms, a peasant woman in a black shawl like those our maquis fighters wore in Corrèze, was shouting, "Why don't they let me through? He said everyone! He said everyone!" I touched the shoulder of one of the marines: "You should let her through: it would please the General. She has the voice of France." He pivoted without a word, and though his hands never moved he seemed to present arms to poor faithful France—and the woman hurried limping toward the church, ahead of the rumble of the tank that bore the coffin.

* *L'Ordre de la Libération,* created in London in 1940 by General de Gaulle, for distinguished activity in the cause of the liberation of France from the Germans.

"Free man is not envious; he willingly accepts what is great and rejoices that it can exist."

—Hegel

Colombey,

Thursday, December 11, 1969

I The fatigue of his last days in power had faded. General de Gaulle turned one of the leather armchairs. His tall figure, a little bent now, dominated the small room where a wood fire blazed. He sat down against the light to protect his eyes, behind a solitaire table with boxes of cards on its green cloth. Never in the dazzling days had I attended an Élysée dinner in the Salon d'Honneur, gilded like the palaces of the century before, without feeling it veer into nothingness, tables laid for two hundred and fifty, musicians under the tapestry of Raphael's "Heliodorus," Mozart's music, and the late-Hapsburg procession . . . Khrushchev, Nehru, Kennedy in the Galerie des Glaces at Versailles, and the restored Trianon, already haunted by departure. . . .

As I shook his hand, I discovered afresh how small and slender were the hands of this man who was still so large. Mao Tse-tung's scalded hands also seem to belong to someone else.

After the words of welcome, we passed into his study. Was the nobility of this room due to the harmony of its proportions with those of the desk, or to the three windows behind him; to the impression of space produced by the books against the wall—the complete works of Bergson, a friend of his family, and mine, which he indicated by a flicker of the eyelids—or to the General, a single armchair opposite him, before the immense landscape black and white from the snow covering the whole of France?

He had said to me in the past, as we walked through the park, "Look, all this was inhabited until the fifth century; and now there isn't one village as far as the horizon." The cell of Saint Bernard, looking out over the snow of centuries, and solitude. . . .

"This time," he said, "it may be finished."

I remembered the sitting room of the Hôtel Lapérouse in 1958, during the general breakdown: "We must know whether the French want to remake France, or take to their beds. I cannot do it without them. But together we can bring institutions to life, gather around us what used to be called the Empire, and give France back its nobleness and its rank." Then he had spoken with dauntless strength, while his tone now was like that in 1941 when he had said of Italy, "Will there be nothing left of her, as Byron put it, but the sorrowful mother of a dead Empire?"

He looked at me gloomily.

"When I have gone, perhaps the age will have played out its role. It's possible. But, you understand, I had a contract with France. Things might have gone well or ill, but she was behind me. She was with me all through the Resistance; there was no doubt about that when I reached Paris. I was sustained by a gigantic wave, and over it I steered my ship. In London, I watched politicians, intellectuals, soldiers, Kanakas* arrive. And after them came the

*Aboriginal people from the French possessions in the Pacific.

gallant seamen from the Isle of Sein:* they were France. When Frenchmen believe in France, oh, yes, then . . . ! But when they stop believing in her. . . . You remember the Pope's remark: 'The French do not love France.' There you are!

"The contract has been broken. Therefore, it is no longer worth anything. This contract was fundamental, because it had no form; it never has had. With no hereditary right, without a referendum, with nothing, I was led to take on the defense of France, and of her fate. I answered her mute and imperious cry. I have said it, written it, proclaimed it. What now?"

Extremely bent, he was alone before the snow which covered the empty stretch of country. "I had a contract with France . . . ." Why did he say France, and not the French? However, he continued, "The French no longer have any national ambition. They don't want to do anything for France. I entertained them with banners, I persuaded them to be patient while waiting for—for what, if not for France?"

He was twenty-four years old at the declaration of war, and I had always wondered whether what he called national ambition was not identical with the will to revenge of his adolescence. . . . But he went on, "Even the English no longer have national ambition."

Attempts have often been made to describe him through psychology. Where he is concerned, such attempts seem vain to me. He was shrewd and even, sometimes, clairvoyant. "One day they will latch on to my coattails to save the country." But his intelligence has more to do with the level of his thought (what Chateaubriand called the intelligence of greatness of spirit) more than from that thought itself or from insight, although he

*A small island off Brittany, population about 1,000. In June 1940 nearly all the able-bodied men left their island to join the Free French in London.

had these; and his intelligence owed something to its obsessive quality as well. I imagine that the great Christians of the Middle Ages, Saint Bernard for example, must have had this kind of intelligence of vocation. The General was haunted by France as Lenin was by the proletariat, as Mao is by China, as perhaps Nehru was by India. Would he explain himself one day? He was not the first to say "France is a person"; that was Michelet. But when Michelet attacked the last Bourbons, when he disparaged Napoleon, he called France to account. General de Gaulle had always done that. For him, she existed as the Church did for those who defended it—or attacked it. The first sentence of his *Mémoires de guerre* is dedicated to her, and I believe that in his heart France had always been less simple than the legendary princess he used to talk about. He was wedded to her before Yvonne Vendroux. However lofty his drama, it was like those of Communist leaders who left the Party. And General de Gaulle was a thousand miles from thinking that France had betrayed him for his successors: she had deceived him with fate—and perhaps with the French.

"But," I said, "in every fundamental thing you have done, weren't you always a minority?"

Each time he had taken charge of France, had he not been? Wasn't he on the eighteenth of June,* and many times with Churchill, and certainly vis-à-vis AMGOT† and Eisenhower's forces, and between the parachutists in 1958 and the marchers from the Place de la Bastille to the

*On June 18, 1940, De Gaulle broadcast over the BBC a call to rally the French people to the defense of France.

†Initials of Allied Military Government of Occupied Territory, a form of government set up in Italy as the Allies fought their way up the peninsula. The Allies (in particular the Americans) proposed to set up AMGOT in France as the country was liberated. De Gaulle forestalled this plan by establishing personal control of the Provisional Government of France, and French civil government was restored immediately in one area after another as it was freed from German occupation.

Place de la Nation? He cordially agreed that all this was true. In comparison, how important was a referendum about regional government and the Senate? Perhaps the French were acting like idiots at that moment, but what else had he done all his life but compel them finally to acknowledge France?

He said, **"I was in a minority, I agree. I knew that, sooner or later, I should cease to be so."**

For a long while I had wondered what the French meant to him. Something that varied, no doubt, like nearly everything deep. The **"gallant seamen from the Isle of Sein"?** To his eyes, they had been the delegates of France (besides, they had reached London with the Kanakas). The women who had taken it for granted that they should house our radio transmitters in the rooms where they worked as dressmakers or typists, knowing that they risked being sent to Ravensbrück? The crowd in the villages after the landing, the crowd at Bayeux, in the Champs Élysées? The crowd that met him everywhere he went on his journeys as President? His link with so many centuries? He called French those who were determined that France should not die.

I thought of the servant girls in Baulieu listening to the declaration of war over the radio; of my companions in the tank—Bonneau the pimp with his wounded finch, Pradé and his youngster, Léonard the fireman from the Casino de Paris who was the stars' beloved; of the men of the maquis, of the women in black shawls each before her grave when our dead in Corrèze were being buried; of the landlady of the hotel at Gramat; of the Mother Superior of the Villefranche convent; of the prisoners of Saint-Michel at Toulouse who, when the Gestapo fellow came into our cell bawling, "Terrorists!" answered in a professorial tone, "Tourists!"; of the youngsters of Ramonchamp and Dannemarie who came with their teacher in the night to plant their little flags on our first graves, or to lay them over our dead without graves.

"Did you judge the contract to be broken in May, or earlier, at the time of your re-election?"

"Much earlier. That's why I took on Pompidou."

What did he mean? At the time of the parliamentary struggle? On his return from Afghanistan? (Then he would have said "kept.") He was not alluding to the time when he called Pompidou to serve, for that would obviously have been wrong. He went on, **"In May, everything was slipping from me. I had lost my grip on my own government. That changed, of course, when I appealed to the country at large, when I said, 'I am dissolving parliament.' "**

"But not for long!"

"Participation, you see—I felt it would be a way of awakening the country, of making it aware of its own existence, of shaking it up! But it had already made its choice. And action is only valid in relation to circumstances which never recur."

"I hadn't much faith in the alliance of capital and labor, hence in participation. . . ."

"You have stood up for both a great deal."

"For the reason I gave you, General: I believe in what Saint-Just called the 'force of circumstances.' The moment you entered on a real struggle with capitalism, the consequences of that struggle would have been incalculable. It is a little like the call of the eighteenth of June, the *Paix des Braves,** or the Community.† As for Marxism,

*"Peace of good men": On October 23, 1958, De Gaulle offered amnesty to all Algerian rebels who would surrender and invited the FLN (the Algerian National Liberation Front) to send representatives under safe conduct to negotiate *une paix des braves* with the French government. The appeal produced no response.

†The French Community of States *(La Communauté)* covering France and those of her colonies and dependencies which voted in favor of the recommendations put forward in a referendum held in 1958. Only Guinea voted to leave the Community in the referendum; other countries left it later.

I spend my time saying to my Left Wing Gaullist friends, 'Get it into your heads that for the General the word *rassemblement** is the symbol of his hopes. I have never seen him so pleased as when some idiot or other yelled that we stood for capitalism, and I answered, "You've been to the Vél'd'Hiv?† Yes? Well, that's not capitalism, that's the subway!" The General is obviously no supporter of capitalism, but neither is he of the proletariat. When he accepted nationalization for some industries it was not to gratify the Communists: to his mind, those nationalizations were an instrument for reviving France. He agrees with Marxism on collective (he would say national) ownership of the means of production, but not on the exaltation of the class struggle.' Isn't that so?"

"Yes."

"The social problem certainly hadn't disappeared, but it had become subordinate—because it had become subordinate the world over."

"Social justice is founded on hope, on the exaltation of a country, not on lazy comfort.

"Participation was a symbol—do you understand. . . . The standard of living has turned into Pandora's box in every country. It is the focus of half of world politics. And yet it isn't the only thing involved. Our old agricultural society was transformed when the peasants gained the right to own land. Our industrial society will be transformed in a similar way. Tentatively participation was the path to this transformation. And you are well aware that in voting against me, France did not turn away from regional government, the Senate, and so forth and so on: she

*Bringing together. In 1947 De Gaulle formed the *Rassemblement du Peuple français* (**RPF**), a non-party movement for constitutional reform. The largest group elected to the upper house in 1948, and to the Assembly in 1951, it soon sank into insignificance through internal disagreements.

†Popular name for the Palais des Sports: abbreviation of its former name, Vélodrome d'Hiver, winter cycling track.

turned away from what participation symbolized. I said what I had to say. But the game was over."

I had heard his speech to the army in Algeria: **"As for you, pay attention to my words: you are not the army's army, you are France's army!"** And the speech on the destruction of what used to be called the Empire; and the one at Strasbourg, delivered in a freezing wind to a crowd of hostile officers: **"If you do not follow me, all you can become is lost soldiers!"** He had said to me some days earlier: **"Character is above all the ability to disregard insults or abandonment by one's own people. People believe I don't know what it means to lose the sense of brotherhood. Do they think I haven't tasted the poisonous flavor of contempt? They have a lot to learn. But one must be willing to lose everything. Otherwise, what can be done? There is no such thing as half a risk."**

He spoke now with the same firmness, but he chose to stand on the sidelines.

"Why did you resign over so secondary a question as regional government? Because it was absurd?"

He looked at me fixedly. **"*Because it was absurd.*"**

How thoroughly he was the past of France, an ageless face, like the snowcovered forest behind him to which he was wedded now.

There is nothing of Charles in his *Mémoires*, but neither was there in a conversation with him. He was expressing a destiny, and still expressed it when he proclaimed his divorce from destiny. Intimacy with him did not mean talking about himself, a tabooed subject, but about France (in a certain way), or about death.

"You were right," he went on, **"not to leave immediately after my departure. People knew you would leave."**

"The Constitution implied that your successor was not the president of the Senate, but the government—that is, your government. And before the elections, many things might have happened. It was very unreal by the way. . . ."

The unreality had begun earlier. I recalled the last sitting of the council under the General's Presidency: plans for unimportant decrees, acceptance of some prefect's retirement, dispatches. The Minister for Foreign Affairs had finished speaking before noon. The General rose.

"Well, gentlemen, we have finished. . . . Until next Wednesday, then. Unless. . . . Well, in that case, a page in the history of France will have been definitively turned. . . ."

It had been turned.

"At the first sitting of the Chamber after your resignation, for two or three minutes I found myself alone on the Ministers' bench with Couve, and Chaban in the chair, in the dim daylight you remember: none of the deputies dared to be the first to enter. . . ."

At Colombey too the light was unreal, because of its reflection by the snow. I know that kind of white light, for it changes the colors of a painting; but there were no paintings here. On the table lay some leaves of manuscript covered with his upward handwriting: his *Mémoires*, no doubt.

"You're writing the next part of your *Mémoires*, and an ideological book?"

"I'm writing my *Mémoires*, from 1958 to 1962. After that, there will be two more volumes."

"No crossing of the desert?"

"No. People have told you it was ideology because I am not writing a chronological narrative. It will be a simple thing, you understand, like the *Mémoires de guerre*. I tell what I did, and why."

I thought again of the Hôtel Lapérouse in 1958.

He went on, **"How odd it is that a man has to drive**

himself so hard, to tear out of himself what he wants to write! Yet it is almost easy to draw out what one wants to say in speech. Colette used to say, 'The French language is so difficult! The adjectives!' She was mistaken, despite her talent: the French language is verbs. And then to shake off the idiosyncrasies. . . ."

He was alluding to the triple rhythm which obsessed and irritated him. Thus far, he had by no means freed himself from it.

"I'm told you're planning to publish everything you have *said* since the eighteenth of June: speeches and press conferences?"

"Except for the bits to the mayors along the road. But it's good to set things down at the dates they were said."

"Their total effect could be remarkable because the broadcasts you made from London were not speeches, they were monologues intended for invisible crowds. . . . The day the radio poured out a mass of 'personal messages' which quite plainly announced the landing, I thought of the scene in the *Soulier de satin:** 'All you who listen to me in darkness. . . .'

"The special tone of your talks lies in the very fact that they were not speeches. And of course the press conference too was a new means of expression. The writer doesn't know his readers either. And to a certain extent he creates them, as you created your listeners. . . . I think the difference is that every great writer is linked with those who have preceded him, whereas your broadcasts had no precedent. Except one. You remember Vézelay:† the knights standing below couldn't possibly have heard Saint Bernard, for obviously he was speaking without a microphone! Yet they left for the Crusade.

*Play by Paul Claudel (1868–1955).

†Town in the department of Yonne. It stands on a high hill, from which Saint Bernard preached the Second Crusade.

"And there will be surprises: I don't remember finding in the *Mémoires de guerre*, 'It is natural, and absolutely justifiable, that the Germans in France should be killed by the French: all they had to do was stay at home.' "

"Yes. When I have finished with institutions, there will also be—what?—what I have to say. If I write, people will of course want to know what I am thinking, what I thought! And I am going to tell them. I am also going to tell what happened."

I believe that men make institutions rather than institutions men; but I knew that this book, heir to the *Mémoires de guerre*, would be a Roman simplification of events—the simplification by which, in literature as in architecture, Rome imposes its domination so strongly—and it would omit the fact that he had always put many irons in the fire (certain chosen irons) so that, when the day came, he could draw forth the one effective weapon. He was not Latin; he was Roman, which means almost the opposite. Disdainfully, even indifferently, he would set his colonnades of destiny against the gossip in which certain well-informed people would reveal that everyone —except the General—had done everything.

"I like *The Three Musketeers*," he said. **"It is as good as your friend *Puss in Boots*. But their success comes from the fact that the war with England has nothing to do with Richelieu's policy, and depends altogether on d'Artagnan's recovery of Anne of Austria's diamond studs. People want history to resemble themselves or, at least, to resemble their dreams. Happily, they sometimes have great dreams."**

"There exists," said I, "a field of literature which criticism has not singled out because it is confused with memoirs: I mean the books that recount what their author *has done. Not* felt. Memoirs are often resurrections of feelings. An account of the carrying out of a great plan poses other problems. If the *Gallic Wars* were not by Caesar, the book would be neither better nor worse on that account; but it would be of a different nature. If the *Mémorial* had been put together from the reminiscences of Las Cases, if Napoleon had not been speaking in it, it would be another book. Yours has sometimes been attacked, and more often admired. In my opinion, through a misunderstanding. The *Mémoires de guerre* have nothing in common with the *Mémoires d'outre-tombe*,* and it will be the same with what you are writing now. Your aim is not directed to the same target."

In my view, his *Mémoires*, whether the account be that of his upholding France at the time of the 1940 surrender or during the hopeful days of 1958, are a tragedy with two protagonists: the French and himself. In war and in peace, France is the stake. On several occasions, he had played France against the majority of Frenchmen. He derived a bitter and secret pride from this. Did he hope that posterity would understand? Had he now passed beyond this hope, and others? I dreamed of a kind of Oedipus of whom a Sophocles would tell how he had wanted to build Thebes in spite of the Thebans. At Kronstadt, Lenin and Trotsky had been faced by the same drama, savagely resolved: proletarians against the proletariat. He possessed a rare steadfastness, but after all he was a man, and not a character in a play. One evening he had said to me, **"If it had been only a question of going into liquidation, what need was there for me? The Fourth Republic was a good enough finale to a great book of history."** In his *Mémoires de guerre*, a distrustful modesty separates him from the main point, as to which he was nonetheless quite clear. Some days after his return, during the Algiers drama, he had said to me, **"You**

*Famous memoirs by Chateaubriand (1768–1848).

know Colonel Lacheroy, don't you? I have never met him. Send him to me." The colonel was at that time one of the principal officers of the psychological service and a sort of local minister of information, giving press conferences in a Burgundian accent. He came to the Matignon. The General listened to him. "Good. Now Lacheroy, get this into your head: there is no need to defend France against de Gaulle." Exit Lacheroy. "When I spoke at Algiers," said the General to me on that occasion, "everyone understood that this time it was France who was speaking."

He continued, after a silence, "What we wanted (between you and me, why not give it its true name—greatness) is ended. Oh, France may still astonish the world; but later on. She is going to negotiate over everything. With the Americans and even the Russians, with the Germans and with the Communists. It has begun. It may continue, with no great consequences. Barring an incident. France does not anticipate one. Nor do the others either. I do not believe that will last. You will see. Members of parliament can paralyze action; they cannot initiate it. France rose against parliamentarianism: she is going to rush into it again. And it will defend her as intelligently as it did when I was trying to get tanks accepted!"*

"But Hitler is dead."

"The country chose cancer. What could I do about it?"

He had never acquiesced in confusing the country with the politicians, but he had just said the country, and not the politicians.

Grandeur is ended. . . . He had re-established France from a base of faith, and faith does not have only a religious meaning. How did Saint Martin, a Hungarian,

*A reference to De Gaulle's book *Vers l'armée de métier*, published in 1934 and advocating the use of tanks and other armored vehicles. The French and British ignored the book, but it was studied and acted on by the Germans. The first translation in English, *The Army of the Future*, appeared in 1940.

evangelize the Loire provinces? How did the Irish evangelists evangelize Germany? Any faith that implies a vocation, whether in the service of Christ or of France, is highly contagious. His faith in France was not enough to make him General de Gaulle, but without that faith he would have been only an intrusive conqueror among the true believers, or a more or less heroic failure. Defeated Napoleon crumbled under his past victories; but he had been obsessed by himself, not by France. Once again, I saw in the General the quality I have called that of the head of a religious order. France forsook him and he paces his Merovingian wilderness above Clairvaux: he does not think of going to serve the Sultan.* Yet his relationship with France was far from simple. His answer in the old days to journalists, **"But I was France!"** was in the past tense. His reply to Churchill, **"If I am not France, what am I doing in your office?"** seemed to be in the conditional. After the famous call no one believed that he *was* France, least of all he himself. He decided to be her. When he said to the vanquished French, to the astonished world, ***"France exists!"*** who else but he would have dared to say it? The politicians of the Third Republic no longer believed in France. Marshal Pétain was at that time a touching custodian of the ruins, but his custody, far from meaning that France existed, meant that France had ceased to exist. The General knew (it is not enough to say he felt passionately) that the agony of France came not from the lack of reason for believing in her: defeat, demography, secondary industry, etc., but from her *inability to believe* in anything at all. He had said to me once, **"Even if Communism lets the Russians believe in**

*After the failure of Bonaparte's expedition to Corsica in 1794, he was ordered to La Vendée, but refused to go. He subsequently sought permission to go to Turkey to reorganize the artillery of the Sultan. Nothing came of this plan.

Russia for nonsensical reasons, that belief is irreplaceable."

Nehru asked me, more wearily, "Surely it is necessary both to keep our feet on the ground, and our heads well above ground level?" The word grandeur, which the General used so often, and which others have so often taken up for or against him, had come in the end to signify both display, and a theatrical expression of history. Now, the grandeur of this study came from the immense wilderness outside; it was no Versailles. The General's idea of greatness was inseparable from austerity—this was true even at the Élysée receptions—inseparable from independence, and from a harsh rejection of the theatrical. The Shah confided to me, "When I met him for the first time at Teheran, I was a young man. I asked his advice. He answered, **'Your Highness, people will suggest many cunning moves to you. Follow none of them. I have only one suggestion to offer you, but it is important: put all your energy into remaining independent.'** " People often quote **"To be great is to be wedded to a great quarrel,"** because he used this phrase from Shakespeare as the epigraph to *Le Fil de l'épée*.* He said to me, **"Greatness is a road that leads toward something unknown."**

And how many times he repeated, **"When everything is going badly, and you are trying to make up your mind, look toward the heights: no complications there."** Contrary to what his friends, and even more his enemies, supposed, greatness was not a domain that he believed he owned, but a domain which he served, knowing that this domain served him. This was Saint Bernard's attitude to the service of Christ, from whom he expected a good deal. . . . For the General, greatness was first of all a solitude, but a solitude where he was not alone.

*English translation, *The Edge of the Sword*, by Gerard Hopkins, 1960.

"What should I be doing on the Avenue de Breteuil?"* he said. "Perhaps I had a pact with misfortune, and not with this bunch."

"And what about the Liberation, and ten years of resurrection for France?"

"What is happening is not even misfortune. And I shall not be able, a third time, to grab France by the hair at the last moment."

"Do you think that at Colombey you don't loom like the statue of the Commendatore?"†

"Well, you understand what I mean. . . . I shall emerge from my silence only if the country is called into question. People ought to know—and I count on you for this—that I am a stranger to what is going on. It is no concern of mine. It is not what I wanted. It is something else. I don't mean to blame anyone: to blame someone is always a weakness. But the page is turned. Once again the nation will fall to tracing the victories of others on the map and discussing them with great seriousness!"

He reproached his successors with the lack of a great plan, and the world as well.

"President Nixon is still getting applause because Asia still believes peace to be possible. But he hasn't seen the end of that Pandora's box. Every great plan is long-term. Despite its power, I don't believe the United States has a long-term policy. Its desire, and it will satisfy it one day, is to desert Europe. You will see. Russia simply wants to gain time. And France no longer has any plan at all. But I am not writing for those who are going to read me. It is much too early. And when I am dead, at first you will see the parties reappear, with their regime of misfortune, but in the end they will embrace one another."

"When John Foster Dulles came here, you said to me,

*In the Invalides.
†A figure of moral principle and retribution in the Don Juan legend.

"There will no longer be a West.' Obviously Europe need not be the West, but if she must build herself up against the West, I wish her luck!"

"When did the French understand what Dulles wanted? They were with me. They are so no longer. That doesn't mean they are with the others. . . ."

The others. . . . When Trotsky talked of Stalin, he used to call him the Other one. Trotsky and I used to talk at Royan, in his little house buzzing with disciples; his desk was littered with newspapers. Here, the solitude did not spring only from the fact that we were alone. I believe I understood the weariness which the General put into words with a contagious calm; I understood its origin less well. I remembered the Council of Ministers which followed the Évian agreements.* The negotiators had just finished making their report. The General, who usually began by calling on the younger state secretaries to speak, passed from right to left, and this made me the first speaker, not by chance. I said that compensating the Frenchmen of Algeria would cost less than an endless war, but that we had first to decide whether what France meant for the world could be reconciled with this war.

Michel Debré passionately argued his point of view, which Jacques Soustelle had defended with bitterness. We were on the main floor of the Élysée. There was no more rose garden: for how long had destiny been absent? This time, it was a matter not of descending the Champs Élysées, but of a fundamental game which would be played out around the table. We went on talking, talking there before the *motionless* General, separated from the careless passing of the clouds by those green curtains which framed them. When each member had given his opinion—this took two hours—the General said, **"The**

*Agreements entered into March 19, 1962, governing relations between France and independent Algeria.

destiny of France does not necessarily coincide with the interests of the Frenchmen of Algeria."

Accordingly, the Algerian war was ended—and the OAS* attacks were to begin.

Louis Martin-Chauffier asserted that the General had told him in 1958, **"We shall leave Algeria."** To me he said only, **"Algeria will remain French as France has remained Roman. But be careful!"** Like him, I believed then in the *Paix des Braves.* At all costs, he wanted agreement—and took it for granted that he would achieve it. A mistake. But I knew that of the irons that were glowing in the fire, he was waiting to draw the sword of France. During the Melun negotiations,† I heard him say, **"Michel Debré doesn't like it? And do you think I do?"**

Why then, at the time of this incidental referendum, had he seen himself facing an irremediable conflict? The project for the transformation of Les Halles had just shown him the limits of his power as against the local communities, but he was ready for one more fight.

As if our silent thoughts were conversing, he asked me, **"You know that the rats from Les Halles are already at Rungis?"**

I too had been intrigued by the migration of these rats to Rungis, as if their guardian spirit had revealed to them the relocation there of Les Halles. It may have been their departure that reminded me of the interim government's last ceremony at the Arc de Triomphe. The drums beating for the dead had sent the pigeons darting up from Rude's statue of "La Marseillaise" in a last wheeling movement that scattered in the wind. . . .

"Do you read the papers, General?"

* *Organisation de l'Armée Secrète*: terrorist organization formed in 1961 to overthrow the constitutional government of Algeria and set up *Algérie française*. It was responsible for a number of outrages in both Algeria and France.

† Abortive negotiations carried on between the FLN and the French government, June 25-July 1, 1960.

"Oh, the headlines! . . . I have told you: I have nothing to do with what is happening."

"Not even in the world? In the past I have tried to understand the enthusiasm you inspired far away. Canada, Rumania, fine! Latin America, at a pinch. But Shiraz? The people there couldn't have pointed to France on a map. . . . And there was no attempt at propaganda, not even the sort of propaganda that played such a great part in Khrushchev's journey, for example.

"I should like to know what you meant to them. Some of the crowd were shouting, 'Shah in Shah!' and others, so the ambassador told me, 'Long live Roustem!' which would be rather like our shouting, 'Long live Roland!' That is to say, they saw you as the reincarnation of one of their own heroes. But I should like to know what that meant: *who* was General de Gaulle to these people acclaiming him?"

"And it was the same in Indonesia. . . . In Latin America, it was different. Why shouldn't the Spanish like me? They love Don Quixote! But the world too has settled back to its lazy comfort. The mice are dancing. You know, even in France in the best of times, it is always strange when people like you. If you know what I mean."

"Your predecessor, in France if not in Iran, is not a politician—not even Clemenceau: it is Victor Hugo."

"Actually you know, my only international rival is Tintin!* We are the little fellows who refuse to get taken by the big ones. No one sees this, because of my height."

His chuckle stretched into a tired movement of the shoulders. In the past, Einstein had said to me of Gandhi, "The example of a morally superior life is invincible." I am far from certain of this. And the life of General de Gaulle, lofty as it was, was not morally superior, in that

*Child protagonist of a widely read French-language comic strip.

sense. What made him a legendary figure? He was not a great commander; he was not a saint. He was not a conqueror in war, in the sense in which Clemenceau had been. A great politician? But Richelieu, Bismarck are not legendary figures; political giants never are. I had said to him that his France was not rational; but neither was he. There are, of course, several rational elements in the glamour that surrounded him: he had been the liberator, the lone conqueror, the intractable man, the regenerator of national energy and thus of hope, even in 1958; the one man it was possible to pit against disaster, not because he would bring about a "national coalition" in the manner of Poincaré or Doumergue, but because he carried France within himself; the prophet, a little. . . . Of course, he had talent too: when he spoke to the parliamentary assemblies of Great Britain or the United States, he spoke as France. The Presidents of the Fourth Republic would not necessarily speak badly, but no one would have listened to them.

His dialogue with the politicians had always been dialogues of the deaf. The Royalists who, in their writings, opposed Danton and then Saint-Just were certainly not all fools, and the ideology of many of them was less visionary than Saint-Just's. But he was not identified by his ideology: he was identified by the Strasbourg guillotine and by Fleurus. When such and such a politician declared what the General "ought to have done," he was not necessarily wrong; but that does not matter. Any more than the Gaullist ideology itself. What we have so often heard called "unconditional" (for submission to Stalin and his tribunals was totally conditional, was it not?) was in fact the irrational. There is an eloquence of deeds which is not the eloquence of words although it often instigates words: the call of the eighteenth of June belonged to that realm. With a mysterious effect on the world, different from politics. Who in Mexico or at Shiraz knows the names of the General's adversaries? What significance could they have since, for the people of Mexico or Shiraz, they would mean *nothing* at all?

What General de Gaulle meant to those Frenchmen who followed him was plain. Presumably, that he was one of those men without whom France would be different from what she is. But for all the others? For the Third World, he embodied independence, and not only the independence of France. He re-established the France so many nations had once loved, and not a France *über Alles;* he was the defender of Africa and, in the end, of Vietnam. He restored to France a strength linked to himself, and at first to France's weakness; they listened to him, rather than to the giants, because he was in a position to threaten no one. But none of that, not even all of it, explained the enthusiasm of Iran, the respect of Mao —or the Mexican teacher who said to Joxe* when he visited his little museum, "Good-bye, servant of a hero. . . ." The teacher did not call General de Gaulle a hero because he approved of his policy. The personality he called hero belonged to fantasy. The effect he made did not come from the results he achieved, but from the dreams which he incarnated, and which existed before he did. The hero of history is the brother of the hero of romance; a knight is not a *Reiter.*† The crucifixion revealed the regality of sacrifice. Of course, the hero of history does not act so plainly, and his fame often comes from the scattered feelings he commands. Alexander's fame is his own (the greatest conqueror of the Western world), but not Caesar's: it was Caesar's murder that insured his fame. Napoleon's defeat did not destroy his

*Louis Joxe, journalist and politician.

†German *Reiter,* French *reitre,* armed German horseman who served in France in the 16th century.

legend, because Saint Helena made him the fellow of Prometheus. He became Napoleon when he ceased to be Bonaparte, as Michelangelo became Michelangelo when he had ceased to be Signor Buonarotti, as I have said before. And General de Gaulle became that personage when he ceased to be Charles. That is perhaps why, when history was at issue, the General readily referred to himself as De Gaulle. The human race needed to invent the royal portal of Chartres, Ellora, the Chinese grottoes —and the transfigured personages of the Sistine Chapel. In Shiraz, in Mexico, General de Gaulle is undoubtedly a figure from the Sistine Chapel. Mao talked to me of him for a long time; I do not remember that he spoke much of France. Clemenceau was Clemenceau through victory, Churchill was Churchill through the Battle of Britain. The General was not De Gaulle solely because of the eighteenth of June. He was inseparable from certain very understandable qualities (will power, steadfastness, eloquence, etc.), as great commanders are inseparable from military genius, and artists from artistic genius; but he was also identified with forces which seem less his own than destiny's. For his friends, and for his enemies, there was something of wizardry in him (and to the tribunal of Rouen, if Joan of Arc was not bound to the saints, how could she be bound to anything but the devil?). I am reminded afresh of Einstein, his violin under his arm, saying, "The word progress will have no meaning so long as there are unhappy children." Dostoevsky had expressed this feeling more tragically: "If the world allows the torture of an innocent child by a brute, I hand in my ticket."

In the past, I have written that the smallest act of heroism is no less mysterious than the torture of an innocent child. I remember Bernanos's face when I said to him, speaking of the extermination camps, "Satan has reappeared on earth." Our Resistance at all costs (sometimes at what cost!) was the answer to those camps, of which it was unaware: Vercors* was the answer to Mauthausen.† And in this domain General de Gaulle was the answer to Himmler. For us, the French. But for others? At the moment when it was pulverized, the French army had been enjoying a reputation since 1918 as the best army in the world. Was the resurrection of France on the same scale as her disaster? But these matters cannot be expressed in military terms. A type of human being who has no name, who may play a part in history as remarkable as the hero's or the saint's is the man who eludes destiny—and that perhaps is the definition of the legendary man.

The General put his hand on the working sheet of his *Mémoires*.

"Malraux, really, between you and me, is it worthwhile?"

All his friends were dead—and most of mine. . . . He added, **"Why write?"**

"And why live? You know the *Bhagavad-Gita:* 'And what use is power, what use is joy, what use is life?' "

The giant heads of Elephanta in the half-light, the strident sea gulls on the tossing crests of the waves in the Gulf of Oman. . . . I had an uneasy sensation of emerging from emptiness, in the face of that snow that would return unfailingly to the earth.

"General, why need life have a meaning? The last time I was in Singapore I met an old friend of mine. He had been director of education in Indochina and began collecting butterflies when he realized death was coming

*Vast plateau in Southeast France, a center of Resistance activity and scene of a major battle between the maquis and the Germans in 1944.

†Extermination camp in Austria where 120,000 deportees from France and other German-occupied territories are estimated to have died.

near. 'Often now,' he said, 'I put myself in the position of the butterflies. . . . They have existed for two hundred and sixty million years, and the average life of a butterfly lasts two months. They know their regions in Malaysia, their islands. In Java, in Bali, they were there long before man. . . . They surely must exchange butterfly stories: the flowers left the trees to become offerings, to deck the hair. . . . Human beings have come one after the other, and have massacred one another, naturally, as they followed one another. Fools. . . . You can be sure that, for the butterflies, the only vaguely serious part of humanity is the women who do not massacre one another. . . . Surely they must say, we have been the same butterflies for so long, and the puny stories of men . . .' "

"And the history of men!"

" '. . . seem so frenzied and irrational. . . .' If the universe is not viewed as a dependency of man, mankind is just one event among many. I quoted to my poor friend from the sacred Indian text the passage where, after the battle, large butterflies 'come to settle on the dead warriors and the sleeping conquerors. . . .' "

"Wonderful sentence! I appreciate that to the butterflies human life may be a brief incident. They do not, however, answer the question you posed, though in certain respects they nullify it."

He repeated, in an ironical and bitter echo (but I never discovered what it was in him that expressed bitterness), **"Why need life have a meaning . . . !"**

How many human beings, in the course of how many centuries, have asked themselves the same question, in small unlighted rooms in Forbidden Cities, or under the sky shared by the queens of Babylon and the slaves of Rome, watching their newborn slave infants die?

He shrugged his shoulders imperceptibly.

"Since they began to think, what answer have the philosophers produced?"

"Doesn't the answer belong rather to religions? If life must have a meaning, it is surely because that alone can give a meaning to death. . . . You remember Einstein's remark, 'The most surprising thing is that the world almost certainly has a sense.' But it does not follow that the world's sense is the same as our life's. . . . And if our civilization is certainly not the first to deny the immortality of the soul, it is the first in which the soul has no importance. . . ."

"Why do you speak as if you believed, since you do not?"

"Renan was not a fool. . . ."

"That depended on the day."

He thought that, in my way, I had faith; and I thought that, in his way, he had not. He said to me, **"There is religious consolation; there is no religious thought."** Even the Hindus, for whom human thought floats ridiculously on the surface of the sacred, would not say that. But he meant what India says. Consolation: that is not the grave of his daughter (which was not unimportant for he had told me, **"I shall be buried with Anne"**); for him it is undoubtedly what is in tune with the surge of the soul which thought confuses with its poor tremor. . . .

He said to me, **"Death: you know what death is?"**

"The goddess of sleep. Dying has never interested me —nor you either. We belong to those people to whom being killed is a matter of indifference. All the same, my relationship with death is far from clear. When the Germans stuck me up against a wall at Gramat, I did not believe I was going to be executed. But in the attack on the La Parère Heights (I think you were on the hill opposite), the mortar shells came over with that whine that seemed to be seeking us out. We hurled ourselves down, and I went on cracking jokes. A bit of shrapnel cut my belt in two. (When you're lying down, that means it hasn't missed by much.) At that, I fell silent. Why? Perhaps because you don't talk to death. . . . It is episodic. But the idea of death itself forces the real metaphysical problem, the problem of the meaning of life. Since I came to feel that death is indistinguishable from sleep. . . ."

"Was that long ago?"

"My basic attitude used to be different, because it was much more a question. My strongest recollection along this line is from Spain, and I remember it precisely because I had a great deal of trouble reproducing it in my film. The Italian fighters bore down on us, in the large sights of that time. I began to fire; the sight shook furiously, and a hideous racket filled the gun-turret of the airplane. An ant ran nonchalantly across the sight I was using to fire on the Italians, who were gunning for me with all their might; ants are deaf.

"So are men, in a way.

"The ants had been totally unconcerned under fire; but when the film was being made, they kept running off. . . . In the end, an assistant director smeared honey on one edge of the sight; the ants made their way toward that, and we got what we wanted. . . .

"How does Islam put it today in the modernized Koran—can an insect crushed on the road by a car apprehend the internal combustion engine?"

A bluish-gray cat jumped on to the desk. Where had it come from? The door was shut.

"Did you know," said the General, his eyelids puckered ironically, **"that at the United Nations there is a black cat no one dares to drive away? Whenever these people discuss the future of the world, the cat walks through and puts things into their proper perspective. . . ."**

As if it felt itself at issue, his cat walked toward him.

"General, do you know how to do nothing?"

"Ask the cat. We play solitaire and take walks together. It isn't easy for a man to force himself into a discipline of idleness, but it is essential. Life is not work: to work without stopping sends a man mad. Remember that. And to want to do so is a bad sign: those of your colleagues who could not stop working were by no means the best."

He stroked the cat absent-mindedly. I said, "Death with suffering and death without suffering may not be the same."

"Unless everything comes together at the decisive instant. If there is a decisive instant."

"One of the greatest minds I have known died of cancer saying to Paulhan, 'How curious death is!' And then the death of those we have loved. . . ."

He turned instinctively in the direction of the Colombey graveyard—it could not be seen from his desk. Behind him the snow was falling. He was thinking, I suppose, of his daughter Anne who is buried up there.

"After a time," he said, **"we think of those we have loved with a sweetness that cannot be explained."**

He had never spoken of her to me, except in a tenderly allusive way. But I believe she played a profound part in his life. In London, it was when he walked holding her hand that he used to reflect, and perhaps the tone of his reflections would have been somehow different had they not been born in the presence of pain.

"It is not true," he went on, **"that our deepest experiences rule our life. In action, yes; otherwise, no."**

"The experience of a return to life, which was so familiar to me after Sheba and again after my pretended execution during the Resistance—that sense is beginning to fade in my memory. . . ."

"The worst misery fades away. But of course our idea

of death is only significant because of what it does to our ideas about life."

"You know the famous expression, 'Life is the totality of the powers that resist death.' And that comes back to saying that death is the soul of the world, and seems to me pure verbiage. There is certainly a problem about our own death, but that is because we are alive. And it is not necessarily the problem of death. Confronted with faith, it is different. . . ."

As always when I spoke to him of faith—which meant his faith—he made the slight gesture that seemed to chase flies away.

"Kittens play; cats meditate," he replied.

I should have liked to stroke the cat sitting on the desk. I answered, "Or seem to. Children, men meditate, or pretend to. A friend of mine, an eminent psychoanalyst, said to me, 'Life is a fellow on the subway carrying a suitcase in each hand. He is frantic, anxious to make the best connections to arrive as quickly as possible—at what final station? At death. But he hangs on to his luggage with all his might. . . .' "

"How old was your friend? His point of view is important, but it isn't a young man's."

"About sixty-five. . . ."

"Yes. Still, he doesn't attach enough importance to ambition. No disease is more widespread. The suitcases are full of it. It is surprising."

"And the desire to be loved is often part of it. Have you noticed that ambition is not counted among the deadly sins?"

"Don't worry, pride and envy cover the subject. What does it matter? For centuries, it was customary after the age of fifty to meditate in the glow death casts on life: the retreat, the monastery. In our time, it has become a matter of preventing the question from being put. There where religion vanishes, knowledge lives for centuries, and the scholar lives from day to day. The image of the suitcases is striking, but life consists not in being obsessed by one's suitcases; it consists in getting rid of them.

"Well, not always. The suitcases let us avoid dealing with things, with the essentials. Do we carry them because of what they hold, or because they allow us to ignore the journey? Ambition apart, what do they hold? It is true, men are very anxious to keep postponing the problems death sets them. And the suitcases are full of the passions of the moment. Some add a certain genius. Death undertakes to calm all this worrying."

"Or to transform it."

"Yes, certainly. Why not?"

"Not everyone who might have liked to could put France in his suitcases."

"I gave France back what she had given me."

Snow.

He went on, shrugging his shoulders, "What is it to get away from the suitcases?"

"Living in the present as you live in history?"

"History may vindicate life; it does not resemble it."

"Like painting. . . ."

"Stalin said only one serious thing to me, and I have quoted it to you before: 'In the end, death is the only winner.' Still, there is contemplation."

He had quoted that remark earlier, and I understood it no more then than I did on this day. But his life for the moment was organized around his *Mémoires.*

"Writing is also a powerful drug," I said. "The suitcases are full of blank pages demanding to be written on. . . . When there is no transcendent idea to draw on, men's most secret and most poignant feeling is often, how can I keep from thinking about the essential?

"In regard to yourself, Napoleon's celebrated remark

to the Old Guard comes to mind, sometimes vaguely, sometimes clearly: 'And now, I will write about the great things we have done together. . . .' "

"He had plenty of luck!"

His ironic voice changed, as if he were returning to an earlier point. **"He believed that posterity might agree with him, with what he thought of his exploits, of what he called his glory. We will talk of this again. Writing allows one to forget the crowd. That is important.**

"Men can live outside all faith. Actually, easier than they can live outside the spirit. There is no doubt at all that Rome created the first atheistic civilization."

"But a superstitious one. When Cicero or someone speaks of the sacred doves, he says he does not like official birds."

"Superstitious like all atheists. No more than that. What did Caesar *believe?* Nothing he wrote tells us that. Nor even anything written about him. And a great deal has been written."

"That is why I think it not unimportant that you are writing your *Mémoires.* If you don't, do you doubt that others will write them? You know that superb reply: 'What is the point, Socrates, in learning to play the lyre, since you are about to die?' 'To play the lyre before I die.' And there is a second reply: look at what is beginning to be said about the events of May. The buzzing over Saint Helena is enough to show that the *Mémorial* is irreplaceable.

"And then, when you are writing, whether you write *I* or *De Gaulle,* the reader reads your own testimony (I refer you again to Caesar's *Campaigns* which always say 'Caesar' and never 'I') differently from the way he would read another's account. The relationship is reversed. Another person would transmit, as a novelist invents; whereas you testify, even if the reader thinks you are mistaken. I repeat: the *Mémorial* is irreplaceable.

"You have said to me, **'The French want to know what I thought of it all.'** The restoration of France, like the Resistance, was not only a series of events. Of course, it wasn't a dream either. But the Allies, especially the Americans, might have regarded the Resistance as a Foreign Legion, an Anders* army: it is you who made something else of it. And of the restoration of France too. A few days after your speech on the eighteenth of June were enough to make it clear that that had been something different from a call to create a Foreign Legion. You said, **'Our immense forces have not yet been put into play; we shall line up the necessary number of airplanes and tanks; and we shall win for the same reasons that we lost.'** It was unanswerable. But no one referred to it, even at that astonishing Council of Ministers in 1940 which was supposed, theoretically, to have dropped Herriot† by parachute into London (what a joke!). The strength of the prophets of Israel lay in the fact that they proclaimed the Truth when everything was against it. The strength of your speeches in June and of all that followed them sprang from the same prophetic certainty. **'When you shall rise up from among the dead. . . .'** "

"The most important things that have been said to humanity," he answered slowly, **"have always been simple things. . . . Religions . . . you see what I mean. . . . And what they engender is unpredictable. . . ."**

Did the bond between two men alone in that small room, so shut in despite the immense white landscape,

*The Polish General Wladyslaw Anders (1892–1970), taken prisoner by the Russians during the Russian invasion of Poland in 1939, spent 20 months in solitary confinement. After Hitler invaded Russia, he was released to form a new Polish corps, which eventually joined the British command in Italy.

†Edouard Herriot (1872–1957), longtime mayor of Lyons and prime minister of France in 1924–5, 1926 and 1932. He opposed Pétain's government, was interned at Vittel, and later in Germany until April 1945.

make for some kind of telepathy? One day he had said to me, about the Resistance, **"I had to sacrifice everything to it: it was France. To what extent did France fall in with it?"**

"Why didn't your wartime speeches give greater credit to the Resistance in Metropolitan France?" I said. "You thought that sooner or later, the politicians would try to play it against you?"

"I gave it a great role."

"In 1944 or '45 when a journalist asked you where the first army's underground forces got their weapons, you said, **'From Africans discouraged by the winter, and from the Americans.'** But there were the arms we took from the Germans: the submachine guns from the Alsace-Lorraine brigade on exhibit in the Strasbourg museum are German."

"I suppose I wasn't aware of that at the time."

"There was something admirable about the last months of the Resistance: we already knew then what was in store for us. After Jean Moulin's* arrest, the resisters really fought in the face of hell."

Had he been afraid that there was a good deal of bluff about the Resistance, and did he want to credit only what was certain? Had he felt that by itself the Resistance could not insure the continuity of France? He said, **"I hear the deepest voice of our people as one hears the murmur of the sea."** He spoke several times of the Gestapo cellars, and the execution posts.

With him I had seen the post shredded by German bullets, terrible totem which brought the whole Resistance exhibition back to the realm of the documentary. He looked at it as I did, but he probably thought there was not such a difference between the Legion and the maquis.

*Jean Moulin, a hero of the French Resistance who was tortured and killed by the Gestapo.

He said to me, **"The Resistance had several motives, even the noblest segments of it. I believe France knows that I was not battling one policy for the sake of Christianity. I was the Resistance *of France* against Germany. It won't be possible for people to forget that I welcomed everyone. If I had not done that, I should simply have been chief of a party in exile.**

"Some people reproached me for determining to take France upon myself: what else could I have done?"

Now he was obsessed by the period when France was becoming France once more, for he was spending hours each day in bringing that time back to life while the foreign press insisted that France lay dormant. Hadn't the past ten years been a final spasm? I thought of the biologists assembled in San Francisco to observe the experiment which was to produce life from matter: the first round had been won; then came the fascinating moment during which it seemed that life hesitated to come to birth —and the eventual failure.

Ilya Ehrenburg, who hated the General, said nevertheless, "From Moscow, France appeared to be following him three steps behind, like Moslem wives." Did he sometimes think that France had made use of him to revive, and to end the Algerian tragedy, and that she had no further need of him thereafter because she wanted nothing more?

"Bir Hakeim* obviously was not Austerlitz, but those who fought there bore witness nonetheless." That is how he thought of himself. But not always. **"I am the character in Hemingway's *The Old Man and the Sea* : I brought back nothing but a skeleton."**

Now in him there was that strange indifference to ac-

*An oasis and track junction in the desert of Cyrenaica, Libya, about 40 miles southwest of Tobruk. During military operations in 1942, it was held by the 1st Free French brigade against repeated attacks by Rommel's forces.

tion of which he had formerly spoken: **"Some men who are greeted with cheers suddenly reject the burden."** (Whom had he been thinking of? Of Caesar? Probably. Of Saint-Just? He did not know a great deal about him, and did not like him.) But is it possible to analyze indifference to action—which, in the man of action, is probably indifference to everything—or is it born of a fundamental feeling whose sources are primarily justifications? Specialists in brain chemistry have been saying this for ten years. . . . Before his resignation, didn't he hear the knell that warns of death? He seemed invulnerable. All the same, behind the skeleton of *The Old Man and the Sea,* I was aware of his determination. He said to me one day, with apparent sincerity, **"You have certainly convinced me."** Next day he did as he had decided, the opposite of our conversation. But in fact he was collecting his speeches; he was answering the women who wrote to him on the feast of Saint Charles, for the first time asking them for their prayers. The instructions given to Madame de Gaulle, in case of accident, were precise. He spoke of death now with sober indifference; hitherto he had spoken of it only distractedly. "He's packing his bags," said someone who knew him well, with distress.

He believed in his retirement. I didn't. What he was writing was the continuation of his life, an act set against the solitude he traversed each afternoon with his cat. **"As far as my gaze reaches, there is no other house. You can walk for hours and meet no one."** Saint Bernard must have walked this empty winter immensity: Clairvaux lies below us. He made a remark, a surprising one from him (though perhaps it expressed some private area of thought), more surprising still because he had spoken thus of Saint-Just: **"Saint Bernard was certainly a colossus: was he a man of feeling?"**

In the direction of Clairvaux, a gardener crossed La

Boisserie; farther away, a plough seemed to lie abandoned, like a monument to Cincinnatus. There was in General de Gaulle a quality which was not that of a Roman or of Washington, nor of the great religious hermits. Refusal was its supreme value. Perhaps the clue to his character was not simply the impulse to say "No," but that he was at ease only when he said "No."

A parcel was brought in, and he opened it: a typescript of *Discours et messages.*

"The first volume?"

"The war. . . ."

Next day at this hour he would be in this room. He would go over again his theory of the Thirty Years' War that began in 1914: "Foch, Clemenceau, De Gaulle: it's all one," and "Our country is in danger of death"; then, on the day after the destruction by the English fleet of the French fleet at Mers el Kebir, "In the name of those Frenchmen who still remain free to act in accordance with the honor and interests of France, I declare that they have, once for all, taken their hard resolve: they have, once for all, resolved to fight." And "Among the soldiers on the march, the world can scarcely hear the distant tramp of some of our men. . . ." He would turn the pages, add some commas. "The France that fights is necessarily France. . . . The cement of French unity is the blood of those Frenchmen who, as Corneille said, have been unwilling to suffer 'the shame of dying without having fought. . . .' " And, "Our army of Africa, its arms rusted but its valor intact. . . ." He would also meet again the tragic shadow of the suicide Hitler, and Vichy, which no longer cast a shadow: "Since cowardice has proclaimed a regime of shame under the pretext of avoiding suffering. . . . These realists who know nothing of reality. . . . Vichy, which holds France by the wrists while the enemy cuts her throat. . . . The shrouds thrown over our dead by the enemy and

the traitors. . . . Those who claimed to govern our country open their mouths only to order her to roll in the mud. . . .”

Page would follow page, describing what had happened each day. “**The greatest glory in the world, the glory of men who have never surrendered.**” And “**In the immense upheaval only those men matter, count, who know how to think, to will, to act, according to the terrible rhythm of events.**” At one moment he would recall the history he had made as Michelangelo remembered the Sistine Chapel; at the next as an unending struggle with the unending procession of shadows. And lunch time would come.

Here it was.

He asked me, “**Are you still reading?**”

While he received Geoffroy de Courcel, our ambassador in London who had been his aide-de-camp in the past, I talked to his present aide-de-camp and to Madame de Gaulle. I no longer felt that she regarded me as the devil. Was it because I had accompanied the General into his retirement, because feminine feelers had come into play, because for years she had been aware, without understanding it clearly, of my relationship with the General, because on this day I was at Colombey, because she sensed my liking for her? (A liking born when I was told that after the assault at Le Petit-Clamart* she had got out of the car without a word, shaking off the splinters of glass that had fallen on her shoulder and setting her hat straight.) She seemed so much younger that I could perceive the young face Captain de Gaulle had loved. Once

*On August 22, 1962, De Gaulle's car was hit by submachine gun fire as it passed through an outlying section at Paris. This was the more serious of two attempts on his life made by the OAS; plans for two other attempts were discovered in advance and prevented.

listless, today she showed a contagious happiness not unrelated to the General's serenity.

She spoke of the Élysée as if it were a concentration camp. "You know, I wonder how even the General managed to put up with it for so long!"

She loved and admired him, but in such a feminine way. "Oh, the General says that, of course, but, you know. . . !"

On the table there were some puzzles, snarled wires that had to be disentangled. "He is in training for Sunday. He can beat all his grandchildren now. . . ."

I looked at the gleaming twists of wire with which General de Gaulle played. . . . Probably because the windows were on the left, the light had lost its intensity.

Last week I received a prize anonymous letter:

> That's what he was, De Gaulle, smallness of spirit, smallness of soul, smallness of heart!
>
> And in addition narrowness of vision, misinterpretation of history, imperviousness to the Latin genius!
>
> France (and not "his" France), the distraught France who saw with him and through him: her defeat in '40 disguised as victory, abandonment of the Empire camouflaged as glory, treachery as honor, ignorance as light; France who saw her army mutilated and mocked, her law bound hand and foot, her culture disintegrated, her people despised; France led by him to total confusion, to desperate disorder, by the flagrant unbearable contradiction between his high-sounding words and the reality; France who saw her children, knife in hand, turn against her while this old man let fall the carnival mask. France threw him out and still hoped!
>
> France would have pardoned everything if there had been in him any greatness, a breath of the epic, or even of madness. She found in her "guide" simply a diplodocus with a minute brain, a man who had nothing of greatness except monstrous vanity, and

> tenacity in paltriness.
>
> In dismay, France looks at this Monsieur Jourdain from the age of Louis XIV: his preoccupation with his abode, his journeys through the provinces, his anachronistic fondness for budgets, and the prizes for excellence, honor, or good conduct which he awards to his collaborators.
>
> At last, finally enlightened as to this megalomaniac as base as he is crafty, France must worry again now over the publication of these books which will pour fuel on half-extinguished passions, which can only displease America, disappoint Russia. . . .

America, Russia. . . . One day he had said to me, **"Not once—you hear me, not once—did I find standing against me a man who represented France, who took France upon his shoulders."** Only Shakespeare has given powerful expression to the hatred roused by great destinies—or rather, by those destinies which still today rouse hatred because they have roused love: like those of Joan of Arc or Napoleon. We all know the songs sung against the Emperor: *Eh bien dis donc, Napoléon; elle ne r'vient pas, ta Marie-Louise!;* and against Louis XIV: *Le vieux soldat rentre au village, épouser la vieille putain. . . .* The insults lavished on Caesar were doubtless descended from insults heaped on Alexander. The writer of this letter —I have received countless others—would, if he had had the courage, gladly have killed General de Gaulle, in the name of Pétainism while forgetting about Hitler. Some of the more serious Communists would have killed him in the name of the proletariat. Napoleon's enemies never had any difficulty in finding reasons to hate him. And Richelieu, Lenin, Clemenceau: to belong to history is to belong to hatred. Not long before, General de Gaulle had asked me, with his tight smile, **"Don't you find it bizarre to be vilified"** (he never used the word "hated" in referring to himself) **"at one and the same time for what one is, and for what one is not?"**

II As he left his study, he was saying to Geoffroy de Courcel, **"You know, I like our Old Boys, but . . ."**

"But they did stay on!" said Madame de Gaulle.

". . . but people must realize that I have nothing to do with what they do."

Port is served. As in the past, the walls of the drawing room at La Boisserie were covered with paperbound books. Above the shelves stood a dozen miner's lamps and warped photographs of sovereigns and heads of state, reigning, fallen, or dead: Chiang Kai-shek, Eisenhower, Queen Elizabeth II, Kennedy beside Nixon. Paintings (a Marquet among them) which were given him at Algiers. There was nothing not connected with his life; he had bought none of the artwork. A television set: in passing I had noticed another in the Empire drawing room.

We moved to the table.

"And what is happening in Paris? Have you been going about lately?"

His voice has changed. He seems to say: intermission. As it had been at private lunches at the Élysée. When he had left the Presidential office with its enormous globe of the world, he ceased to speak of serious matters. He used to reply with a sentence, often with a witticism. This made his women neighbors uneasy: they were expecting lofty thoughts on the history of the world. Instead, he asked after their children or their opinion on the latest film hit. But at Colombey the General created an atmosphere I had never known at the Élysée: an atmosphere at once domestic and warm, as if he were pleased to find himself master of the house once more.

The ambassador tells us about Baron de Rédé's ball, and the competition in telling anecdotes. "All fairly banal," he said.

"Long live the end of the eighteenth century," said I, "with its dinners divided between the Prince de Ligne's wit in Vienna and Madame de Pompadour's at Versailles! In Vienna a courier comes up, gasping for breath of course, with a message to the Austrian Emperor: 'A man has just drowned in the moat at the Prater!' Waterless moat. 'Come, come, Sire,' says the Prince de Ligne, 'still another flatterer!' You know the rival witticism: Louis XV . . ."

The rest of the phrase would have been ". . . is pawing Madame de Pompadour," but "paw" is a word not in Madame de Gaulle's vocabulary.

"Louis XV is caressing Madame de Pompadour. She takes his hand, places it on her heart, smiles, and says, 'Here it is, good heavens!' "

The cat reappeared. I asked its name.

"It had a very distinguished name," said Madame de Gaulle, laughing, "but I have forgotten it! Now it is called Grigri."

I once asked the General about his relationship to cats. After some reflection, he said, **"They're no longer afraid of me. . . ."**

His niece Geneviève told me that he had been saddened to hear the children in the next room say of the coming Christmas, "If Uncle Charles comes, that'll be fine, but we won't be able to have fun. . . ."

I asked Geoffroy de Courcel, "Have you read the latest English theory about Agincourt?"

"I don't think so."

"According to tradition, the French archers couldn't use their bows because they had no covers for them, and the strings had been slackened by rain, whereas the English archers had covers."

"That's what I was taught," said the General.

"The new theory is this. At that time Europe was overrun by immense swarms of rats. Only the English had companies of cats. One of these rat swarms skirted the English army, not through fear of the cats but because of their odor. And they leapt on the greased strings of the French bows."

"At Agincourt," the General asked, **"did the archers fight with bows or with crossbows?"**

"In the film, with bows. . . . Perhaps it's all nonsense, but an historian could check if the English army did in fact have companies of cats. I like the idea: a hundred and twenty cats in rows. . . ."

"To persuade two of them to live together is difficult enough!" says Madame de Gaulle.

"The cat story I like best," said I, "—I'm no longer sure whether it is Louise de Vilmorin's, Jean Cocteau's, or mine—is this: An old Englishman, his wife, and their black cat are sitting by the fire. The cat looks at the man and says to him, Your wife has deceived you. The Englishman takes down his rifle and kills his wife. The cat goes out, its tail curled in a question mark, and says, I was lying."

"The story sounds like yours," the General says. **"But animal corps have existed for a long time, whether of cats or not."**

"You may recall that some years ago the Archives received a letter in which Charles de Batz, that is to say d'Artagnan, captain of the aviaries, thanked the King for having nominated him captain of his small dogs.

"When all the cats had disappeared from Europe, someone sent an Abyssinian cat to Pope Gregory I, and some ecclesiastical council deplored the fact that the Holy Father neglected his pontifical duties to stroke it."

I remembered a black cat lying on a mouse trap in the "old town" of Concarneau.

On one of the walls of the anteroom, bare twenty years ago, there hung Polynesian clubs, some very beautiful, others the kind made for the tourists. **"That amuses the children,"** said the General.

In the dining room, on a Normandy cupboard, stood sculptured groups from the Far North.

"Eskimos?"

"They were given to us in Quebec," said Madame de Gaulle.

Two maids in white aprons serve the meal. The General himself pours the wine. Until now, I had observed that downward smile and that crinkled eyelid of his only when they accompanied sallies—like the time he said to me, when he saw Brigitte Bardot arriving for a reception at the Élysée, dressed in a frogged pajama-suit, **"Look at that! A soldier!"** To her he said, **"What luck, Madame! You are in uniform and I'm in mufti!"** On another occasion, he was shaking hands with people in a crowd without having put on his spectacles, and said, **"Good day, vicar!"** "But, General, I'm one of the gorillas."* **"Then good day, Mr. Gorilla!"** And more bitterly, to an idiot who said in his presence, "The conditions of detention in Ravensbrück have been exaggerated," **"Sir, the women**

**Gorille:* slang term for security agents or bodyguards.

resisters were so comfortable in the extermination camps that all but a few of them stayed there."

The General asked the ambassador for news of his English friends.

"The most moving letter I received about my resignation was from Mrs. Churchill."

He turned toward me. "Do you know whom the first one came from? From Franco. He invited me to come to Spain."

A roast followed the sole. Excellent Bordeaux. The General never let a glass remain empty. Filling mine, he asked me, "So you didn't go to Algiers?"

I had been invited to preside over the French-speaking Congress there.

"I nearly accepted the invitation: that they asked a Frenchman was significant. I am told that the confusion hit a fever pitch between the American Blacks and the African Blacks. . . ."

"Perhaps you would have put the meeting to rights."

"I could go back into politics only if it meant going back into action. Besides, I feel that I said what I had to say at Niamey. . . ."

"You certainly said some useful things at Niamey. Has the Niger changed much?"

"Less than Chad. Niamey is still a town of the old French Empire where the President lives in the Governor's yellow palace. . . ."

"And the villages?"

"Timeless. But some of our women ethnologists are living in them, and the contribution of these women, in the Islam of the Niger, is irreplaceable. They think they can play some useful role between the Niger and France, and I agree. The village itself has not changed. Except for one thing. All the tall men are called Gaul, as in the Congo —and the Fula are a tall people. Their wives and fiancées are called Tante Yvonne: *tantivonn.* And *Le Canard enchainée* doesn't get to them! So along the goat paths above the river you can hear distant cries of 'Gaul! Gaul!' or 'Tantivonn! Tantivonn!' "

Madame de Gaulle laughed.

"What are the ethnologists doing?" she asked.

"Studying the Nigerian woman. Their work is not easy. The one who acted as my guide has wavy hair. The people of the country have frizzy hair, and for them the river Niger is a goddess with wavy hair, because of the undulations of the waves. The first time this ethnologist went bathing, all the villagers took flight. She went back there some days later, and her best friend told her, 'It's a good thing we knew you well; otherwise they would have killed you. Since you're not the goddess, you could only be a demon. . . .' Since then, she hasn't gone bathing except in a cap, and she covers her hair with a scarf. . . ."

On a cabinet lay several numbers of the *Journal de la France.* The early ones were devoted to the Revolution. The General's glance followed mine.

"Perhaps things were not as difficult as we suppose. France had twenty-eight million inhabitants, and conscription. By the time it ended, the monarchy had rebuilt its military power; the reforms Guibert had demanded were put into effect by the Revolution and the Empire. But the Revolution pushed France back into war, and France has always been shaped by strokes of the sword. And then, battle has that virtue of ennobling even the least pure.

"Who would have believed that the disciples of Jean-Jacques Rousseau would turn into Romans?

"When we went to see the new production of *Ruy Blas*, I said to you, 'What a curious subject,' and you answered, 'To the audience of the time, the valet as the queen's favorite was Rousseau in the position of Prime Minister.'

I hadn't thought of that. Would he have wanted that? Possibly: he was a little mad. . . ."

"Victor Hugo did not know that Maria Ana of Neuburg, the queen in *Ruy Blas,* had a natural son who turned out to be the most extraordinary adventurer of the century, the Comte de Saint-Germain. Cagliostro and Casanova tried to find out by what cunning he managed to get himself received in Louis XV's private apartments, where they never had access; but like all the rulers of the period, Louis XV knew his lineage. . . ."

On the cover of another number of the weekly, there was a large portrait of Napoleon.

"What do you think of the Emperor?" the General asked me.

"A very great mind, and a rather small soul."

"But that wouldn't have been the right thing to say in Corsica. . . ."

I was to have spoken at Ajaccio to commemorate the Emperor's birth, and at the Invalides, the General was to mark the return of his ashes to Paris.

"It seems to me," I said, "that he never faced metaphysical or, if you prefer, religious questions. Read the *Mémorial.* We always hear about his superstitions—as if so many of the greatest religious minds were not superstitious! But his religion, his real religion, must have been fairly akin to his mother's. Great conquerors rarely ask themselves the meaning of life—Alexander, Caesar, Genghis Khan, Tamerlane. . . . When they come before God, I suppose he sends them all to catechism class. . . ."

The General answered, with the half-smile that seemed to mean one more encounter with human oddity, "He had not time for the soul. Consider, at Saint Helena. . . . When did he make the remark I have quoted, 'Yes, it is sad; like greatness. . .' ?"

"When he came back to the Tuileries, after Elba."

"His was no ordinary soul."

The General was much more preoccupied by history than by religion. I share his preoccupation, but not completely. He had said to me in the past that he agreed with Valéry's remark, that the lessons of history have never been of any use. Perhaps the history that obsessed him was less destiny than the presence of the past. Men obsessed by women speak the more of them the more enigmatic they find them. Nevertheless, what he said is true. Spirituality was always foreign to Napoleon, but at Saint Helena his relation to life was not what it had been at Austerlitz.

"And then," he went on, **"in an historic personality, the legendary creative power—you understand what I mean—takes the place of the soul."**

"What would you have said, at the Invalides?"

"He left France smaller than he had found her, granted; but that is not what defines a nation. For France, he had to exist. It is a little like Versailles: it had to be done. Don't let's sell grandeur short."

He knew that strength is strength, and felt France's weakness despairingly; but he did not conceive of France in terms of strength (he thought idiotic Stalin's remark: "France has fewer divisions in line than the Lublin government"*, and even less in terms of territories. Then why had he not felt a clearer conscience when he decided to accept Algeria's independence? On that day, he had chosen the soul of France as against everything else, and principally against his own interests. He did not attach much weight to the fact that Napoleon left a muti-

*Lublin, a Polish town 100 miles southeast of Warsaw, was recovered from the Germans by Russian troops in July 1944. A "provisional government" of Poland was set up here under Russian influence (in opposition to the exiled Polish government in London).

lated France: in his view, the Emperor had proved to Frenchmen that France existed.

"**And then, you know,**" he went on, "**Napoleon's is not the only historic destiny shot through with mistakes.**"

"Every man of history gathers together his weapons before choosing the one he will use."

"**Still, he has to choose. England's tragedy is to be compelled to choose between the remnants of the Empire at the cost of American supremacy, and fair play toward the Continent. Churchill spent his time handing everything over to the United States, beginning with the West Indies in return for fifty ships the Americans weren't using.* And Napoleon could not choose between the generalissimo and the Emperor. Before Leipzig, he spent hours signing decrees. And yet his army was no longer the French army. How do things begin, how do they shift balance?**

"**As late as 1811, his genius had not faltered. The integrations of many efforts into one, the determination to double the stakes, the passion for risk—all that is the essence of strategy. And in battle, he knew as no one else did how to bring on a rupture in the equilibrium of a situation, and how to exploit it instantly. His will never suffered an eclipse, in triumph or in disaster. Calm under stress is the first gift for command, Voltaire said. In every historic destiny, there is the moment when it all begins. It all began at Lodi.**"

I was thinking, and for you? But I knew the answer. It all began when he stopped thinking about General Weygand, about Noguès,† and the others; when he answered René Cassin who asked him in London, "From the legal point of view, should I regard us as a Foreign Legion, or

*In 1940, the British government gave the United States 99-year leases on certain Caribbean ports, in exchange for fifty destroyers built during World War I and laid up in 1940.

†A Vichy general.

as the French army?" "We are France."

France stood before him: two pine tables.

He went on, "But Napoleon always tried to force fate. Yet, souls have their limits like everything else. From 1813 on, by dint of striking with it, he had broken the sword of France. Once the ratio between the end and the means is snapped, the maneuvers of a genius are vain. Everything he did in the first part of his life—I am speaking of him as commander in chief—was beautifully calculated. Everything he did after the retreat from Moscow looks reckless. I'm well aware that when a lieutenant becomes Emperor, he may think the returned Emperor can still win battles, and then see what happens. But he fought those battles as if he were a different man."

"Josephine Baker, whom you've always liked . . ."

"Poor, good girl!"

". . . used to say that it was easier to become a star again than to become one in the first place."

"As long as you don't see yourself as a star. If Napoleon had not won so many battles, would he have launched Waterloo as he did?"

"In the end, he had no cavalry left; he seemed to go into battle against every rule of his youth. . . . Yet Prince Schwarzenberg told me that his own ancestor had managed to bring the Austrian cavalry back from Russia. . . ."

"It may not have been under much attack! But consider how little his defeats have dimmed Napoleon's fame. Look at the might of his name, and not only among the French. He stirs souls. You've been to his tomb: where else do we see the crowd experiencing that thrill of greatness?"

"To the indignation of Tolstoy, who thought him a bandit. After his defeat, Southern France hated him passionately. At Carcassonne, an enormous pyre was made of everything bearing his image, and the people brought a caged eagle to burn alive on the pyre."

"How many men are worth the burning of an eagle out of hatred for them?"

"Do you know what gives me pause when I think of him? His reaction—probably surprise—the first time he lost a battle. . . . You said once you were overcome by Joan of Arc's cry when the flames reached her, because she had been sure, you used to say, that the saints would protect her and that she would not burn. Something of the sort must have happened to him."

"One of his remarks has always troubled me because it is splendid and incomprehensible: 'I make my plans out of the dreams of my sleeping soldiers.' "

"He re-established order—or rather, he established it, for it was not the same order. He had in him the need to transform confusion into order, like all men of history who are not theatrical figures. . . . Politically, this is clear because the confusion he brought to order is clear. But in areas that are not political, the thing becomes more complicated. I am gathering together the essays I wrote once on certain people in the late eighteenth century—thus on one of the most profound crises the individual has ever undergone. What sort of literature would have developed from Laclos, what sort of polity would have developed from Saint-Just? What style of painting would have developed from Goya? It is because of Napoleon that Madame Récamier on her couch followed the 'Maja Desnuda.' But he threw France back into the hands of men. Since 1750, Europe had been conquered not by French men, but by French women."

"He made France mad with ambition. In this domain, the Revolution had been a fantastic tale. He transformed the National Convention delegate into the prefect. As Barrès used to say, he was professor of ambition and professor of energy. But of ambition much more than of energy."

"Saint Rastignac?* You have written, 'The tough spring of ambition which sustains the man of action,' or something of the kind. . . ."

"It's not the passion for rank and honors, but the desire to influence great events. Individual ambition is an infantile passion. Prefer what you appear to what you are, when you are Napoleon! And able to dominate the loneliness of Saint Helena! It isn't simple. Yet, did he have the vocation for France? He loved the French army because at that era and under his command, it was the best. But I believe he conceived his destiny, even on Saint Helena, as that of an extraordinary individual. Yet any individual counts for very little as against a people."

"He is certainly Rastignac's patron saint, General; but he is Nietzsche's too. On Saint Helena, whatever happened, his ambition was fulfilled. Stendhal said that if he had built Italy in 1813, he could have continued the war there after Waterloo."

"He thought in terms of Italians, but not of an Italy. Meanwhile, there was a France already.

"He wasn't always at his best, I know. But he always had against him apathetic elements at home. They count for a good deal."

A vague gesture which seemed to mean, can we reproach men for being sick?

"You're familiar with Malmaison, of course, General. And you, Madame?"

"Oh yes!"

I don't believe I had heard a woman say "Oh yes!" since the Sister Superior of the convent of Villefranche when I asked her if she had the Gospel according to Saint John.

"The arbor where the First Consul played prisoner's

*Eugène de Rastignac, a character in Balzac's *La Comédie humaine*.

base is still there," said the General.

"Opposite the garden gate there was a tree with two great branches. On his return from Austerlitz he had seen his star between them. When he went to Malmaison after Waterloo, it was certainly not in memory of Josephine: she had received the Czar there. It was, says General Bertrand, to find again the star that had disappeared since Smolensk. Napoleon told the story on the ship that carried him to Saint Helena. 'But was it the same sky?' asked the captain. Austerlitz took place on the second of December, Waterloo on the eighteenth of June. The Emperor hadn't thought of that. You can imagine him, diverted from the sky and forgotten by it, silhouetted against the lamps of the corridor of Malmaison, looking for his vanished destiny—and a few days later, the *Bellerophon.* Prince Napoleon, when I told him the story, went to have another look at the garden; but the tree was too old: it had been cut down."

"Who could find his star again, if he set out to look for it?"

" 'Tell us about him, Grandma—tell us about him . . . !' He gave the people the chance to attain to aristocracy, the famous marshal's baton in every soldier's knapsack. But what he called his glory, and placed so high above himself, had a different nature."

"He wanted to make the French an aristocracy, but that's just what they like! And who loved him, if not the people?"

"What is the people, General?"

"France."

The same expression at the time of the second Presidential election, in the Élysée office, with the paintings he used to call "naked women amid morning-glories," the enormous world globe, and the windows framing the now desolate rose garden.

"Of course," he went on, "I hardly believe in the law of numbers; but collective passions exist in minorities as well. I prefer the passions of France to those of the Economic Council, or of the French Academy. Multitudes have had great passions, and even good ones! Corporate bodies are indispensable, but passions are worthless to them: they mistake them for reason.

"Napoleon came to be considered a man of genius by nearly all his foreign enemies. For us, I understand it: he stated positively to France that she was worth more than she believed. And what did we do but that? But for the Germans? The successor of Charlemagne?"

"Nothing is more mysterious than the metamorphosis of an historical biography into a legendary life. Why is Caesar one of the greatest figures of the West? A few victories, important but not fundamental; a great period of government like some others. But there was Plutarch. And Shakespeare."

"He appealed to them; Pompey didn't. Neither did Augustus. Victories are less important than people imagine. Turenne inspired greater respect than did Condé, although why is not clear, for none of his battles is as important as Rocroy. Maurice de Saxe, who never lost a battle, is nothing like the equal of Napoleon who in the end was beaten. Victories that are only victories do not lead far. Something else must come into play. The nation-to-be (Joan of Arc), the future of the world, the confused and symbolic meaning of those who make history? You see what I mean. . . . As to Napoleon, I wonder if the French do not have some obscure sense that, except for Waterloo, he was victorious when he commanded the French army, and was beaten when he commanded the *Grande Armée* which was no longer solely French.

"It seems to me that, without fully realizing it, France is grateful to him for what he *made* of the French. They had recovered from Rossbach.* There had been the soldiers of the year II, ah yes, yes, but they went off when he reached Italy! . . . He made of the French army what Rome made out of the legions, what Alexander made out of the hetaeria. In the end, the thirty-seven thousand men of the Guard were simply Frenchmen, including the Marie-Louise contingent,† who didn't know how to load their guns. Victor Hugo's picture of these poor conscripts mixed up with the Old Guard is a bit of genius. . . ."

I quoted,

> Tranquille, souriant à la mitraille anglaise,
> La garde impériale entra dans la fournaise.‡

"Yes. He wanted to invent a knighthood: Chevaliers of the Legion of Honor. And he created French elite troops that none could resist: 'Murat, the Pratzen plateau is covered with batteries: go and take them.' Believe me, France has not forgotten him, whatever she may think. In 1940, he was behind me when I told the French they were not what they seemed to be. . . ."

He made a vague gesture as if he were reproaching himself for having, during lunch, talked of serious things. He went on, in an almost ironical tone, "And what about your plan for moving l'Aiglon's body?" §

I had thought it absurd that his coffin, by the grace of Hitler, should seem to rival those of our great commanders. Since he had reached the Invalides, however, I wanted him to be placed at the foot of the Emperor's tomb.

*Battle of the Seven Years' War, fought 1757, in which Frederick II of Prussia decisively defeated the combined German and French forces.

†*Les Marie-Louise:* the 1814 conscripts called up under an order by the Empress Marie-Louise.

‡Calm, smiling at the English grapeshot, the Imperial Guard advanced into the furnace.

§The son of Napoleon I and Marie-Louise. Called Napoleon II, he never reigned.

"The move has taken place, I believe. . . ."

"It was barely noticed. But then we don't notice much any longer."

"Why the devil," he resumed with vague curiosity, "have so many insurance companies taken the eagle as their emblem?"

"Because the parent companies were American, I suppose."

"It's curious, this mania the French have for what is foreign! Every evening, the radio talks to me about the Avenue du President Kennedy. So far as I know, there is no Clemenceau Avenue either in London or in Washington, is there?

"It was Johnson who received you in New York?"

"In his capacity as Vice President. With great dignity."

"Yes, of course. . . . Although he never took the trouble to seem to think."

"It was at the Waldorf where the Americans lined the streets to cheer you in 1944. . . ."

"They showered me with scraps of paper, like confetti, along some avenue. An ardent people, and with no vileness to them. That's not bad."

"You remember our conversation, when you came back from the President's funeral? You were speaking of Mrs. Kennedy. I said, 'She played a very intelligent game. Without mixing in politics, she gave her husband the prestige of a Maecenas which he would not have achieved without her help: the dinner for the fifty Nobel prize winners. . . .'"

"And the dinner for you!"

"They were her doing. But you added, 'She is a brave woman, and very well brought up. As to her fate, you are mistaken. She is a star, and she will end up on the yacht of some oil baron.' "

"Did I say that? Well, well! . . . Actually I would sooner

have thought she would marry Sartre. Or you!"

He had resumed his bantering tone, so different from the other, and so special in him, for it never seemed altogether at one with what he was saying. I continued, "You remember the signs in Cuba: 'Kennedy, no; Jackie, yes'?"

"Charles," said Madame de Gaulle, "if we had gone to Cuba, would there have been signs saying 'De Gaulle, no; Yvonne, yes'?"

He rarely answered humorous questions. And humor apart, I was well aware of his bizarre shrewdness. When one of our women friends entered the Carmelite Order, I wrote an article of farewell. He said to me, "Don't publish it: she can still leave the Order. She hasn't taken her vows." She did leave it.

I asked him, "What impression did Indira Gandhi make on you?"

"Those fragile shoulders on which the huge destiny of India rests—and they don't shrink from the burden! Besides, what does it matter? Do you think that if we had had the atomic bomb before the Americans we should have adopted this policy which isn't a policy? When Bonaparte was thrown over by the Directory he might well have made a bad bargain with the Sultan. Born a little farther north, Bourguiba might be mayor of Marseilles. On the whole, women think of love, and men of gold braid or something of that nature. Beyond that, people think only of happiness—which doesn't exist."

I was reminded of his remark, "The illusion of happiness, d'Astier, is for cretins. Have you ever been happy? It must have been a long time ago, I imagine!" But I was reminded at the same time of Gide's phrase, "It's curious, my dear fellow, the trouble I have not being happy!"

I answered, "Women think of love, certainly. But . . . a sensitive woman would have told Stendhal that to crystallize is just an action like any other; whereas to be crystallized is fascinating. . . ."

Madame continued her teasing. "All the same, Charles, you did give them the right to vote."

"France cannot be divided."

"And you pardoned all the women condemned to death."

"Women are capable of the best and of the worst. Therefore they should never be shot."

Did his tone imply: they are irresponsible? Imperceptibly.

"Why is feminine beauty always to some extent a mask? Strange! Greek statues, Italian pictures, films. . . ."

"Make-up. . . . Those I have had the honor to receive with you—Marlene, Ludmila Tcherina, Brigitte Bardot—didn't arrive at the Élysée in curlers. Artists invent the dream; women embody it. But Christianity alone invented the Eternal Feminine."

"Why?"

"I have tried to understand how the 'Venus de Milo' was transformed into a Gothic Virgin. There was one early event that made me muse. When the Church thought its fate depended on Clovis, who was a pagan, it sought a Catholic wife for him, and went a long way to find her, for Clotilde was a little Swiss princess. The Church sought not the most beautiful but the most charming wife for him. The great hetaeras were beautiful, brilliant, even dazzling: but they weren't charming. That femininity which seems best defined as gentleness. . . . Much later, the cult of Mary dominated Christianity: nearly all cathedrals are called Notre Dame. You know the theory: when the lords left for the Crusades, the knights—who were dubbed at thirteen, and until that time had known no women except their mothers and sisters, or the peasant girls they slept with—discovered, in the lord's wife presiding at table, a real woman of twenty-five or thirty years old who bowled them over. . . . The implications are enormous! It is true that the Eternal Feminine is a phenomenon of the Christian world; but its expression is inseparable from the religious domain. Agnès Sorel bares her celebrated breast in her portrait as the Virgin. The exciting moment in painting occurs when the artist discovered the Eternal Feminine as *other* than the Virgin."

"And that accounts for the glory of 'La Gioconda'?"

"It is the only painting the insane compare themselves to—even the males—the only painting people shoot at. If it weren't protected by bulletproof glass, which gives it a greenish tint, it would have been shot full of holes long ago. The man who stole it took it to Gabriele d'Annunzio, in terror. . . . The police found the frame and studied the fingerprints on it, checking them everywhere. But the thief, Perugio, had stopped working at the Louvre six months earlier. The police never turned up his prints, but they made a routine visit to his room and signed their report on a tablecloth that lay over the panel: out of its frame, 'La Gioconda' is not a very thick panel.

"When we sent it to the United States, it left on the 'France.' When the ship was at sea, the flowers meant for the passengers were distributed. One bouquet of Parma violets was left over, with an envelope: 'For Mona Lisa.' Some canny journalist, thought the captain. But the visiting card was blank. . . .

"Actually, 'La Gioconda' may not be Mona Lisa but Constance d'Avalos; she is wearing a widow's veil, and she's older by twenty years. How old is she? She was hung in the bathroom of Francis I, Louis XIV, and Napoleon: during periods, that is, when Leonardo was not admired. And he, who had always had such troubled feelings about his work—he wrote, 'One day it was given me to paint a truly divine face. . . .' In his lifetime, the face certainly emerged like a revelation, because the rediscovery of antique forms came from statues, and the eyes of statues have no expression, and therefore no soul. In Washington I said something like, 'This mortal woman with her divine gaze triumphs over the sightless goddesses. . . .'

"I might have added that when Leonardo painted Christ—in the 'Last Supper'—he did not attempt to reveal his gaze, but had him looking downward. . . . The world of art that includes the gaze is quite different from the world that does not . . . even when it is a question of the inward gaze, as in Buddhism. . . ."

"A face without seeing eyes is antique sculpture, sleep, or death."

"You like Greek sculpture, General?"

In the library I had noticed the backs of several well-known albums.

"You took me to inaugurate exhibitions which made me stop to reflect—the Mexicans, for example. The only sculpture that moves me is the sculpture of the Middle Ages. I was interested when you wrote that the period of the Crusades produced sculptures of soldier saints, never of knights. Saint George never existed—how did he come to be invented? It doesn't matter: as I said, that kind of sculpture has meaning for me. It is France, too. Other kinds are archaeology.

"Still, what would have become of Greek art if Greece had been beaten at Salamis?"

I was ready with my reply, but I wasn't sure on what I based it. "Athens was crushed by Sparta with no great effect on its art. . . . But it would all have ended with Alexander anyhow. . . ."

He seemed to pull himself out of some reverie saying **"Yes. And at dawn, the wolf ate Monsieur Seguin's goat,** which had fought it off all night.*

"And 'La Gioconda's' reception in the United States was as the papers described it?"

"The day after the speeches, I saw the Washington crowds, black women in mink holding the hands of their little daughters in rabbit fur, standing before the Great Icon. . . . In New York, where people lined up to see it from six o'clock in the morning, a lad of twenty appeared, with his sheepskin jacket bulging as though it concealed a Tommy gun. A detective pounced, frisked him, and a little dog sprang out: 'I wanted Foxy to be the only dog in the world to see the "Mona Lisa"!' confessed the boy hopelessly."

Madame de Gaulle was pleased with him.

"We shall continue to send them paintings," said the General, "and it won't mean the same thing at all. . . . But that wasn't your first journey, the one with 'La Gioconda'?

"I remember your cables during that visit—or rather, the ambassador's. Solid reports; but I knew that the President was hoping to come to terms with me, and to avoid coming to terms on Algeria. What do you think today of your conversation with him?"

"There were several, quite different. The first one, don't let's talk about it. Our ambassador was with me. The President didn't want to seem to change his views, in whatever degree, on whatever topic. He was adamant rather than thoughtful, because in his eyes you were a powerful entity, and France didn't exist at all. Therefore, there could be no agreement about the Congo, no agreement about Vietnam. Then, obviously, Algeria came up. He was very courteous, but also in a way . . . relentless. I said to him, 'Sooner or later, there will be an independent Algeria. With us or against us. Then you will pick up

*Story by Alphonse Daudet, *Lettres de mon moulin,* 1869.

the ball in Africa or in Asia, and I wish you luck.' At first he thought I was talking nonsense, then he made a vague gesture as though to brush the question aside. In any case, the conversation was over, since I had nothing to ask of him. He got up out of the revolving armchair in that immense room where we were almost alone, and as he walked to the door with me, he said, 'Well! Mrs. Kennedy will charm all this away this evening.' (He was receiving me at the White House.) 'And we won't talk about Lafayette!' I answered smoothly, 'And who might that be?' He burst out laughing, the double doors were opened, and the photographers, alert for signs of a clash, shot a picture in which we were hilarious. Laurel and Hardy, in fact!"

"And the evening?"

"Polite talk. I was in one room at Mrs. Kennedy's table, he was in the next room, and we bandied words over the microphone. Mrs. Kennedy had done what she could (and it was a great deal) to make our meeting appear to be bathed in a sort of warmth (he later said, 'It was pretty rough.'). Before the weekend and our exchange of frigates (he adored model ships), he said about me, 'All right —I'm doing it for Jackie.' "

"She struck you as a fine person, I hear?"

Reappearance of the elephant's eye.

"The help she gave the President by proclaiming that she did not concern herself with politics, and by introducing the world of the mind into the White House, cannot be dismissed. Apart from that, you know her as well as I do. Louise de Vilmorin, who has known her very much longer, said, 'She pleases without displeasing, which is rare.' "

"Your next visit was with 'La Gioconda'?"

"That was no problem. American warmth is deep and sincere. The President thought that we French were behaving in a friendly way. And certain events had occurred which you know about better than I do. He thought it was you who was sending 'La Gioconda,' but that I had played some part in it. He was a man sensitive to style. So that time he invited me to his country house. Then, after a pleasant lunch of soft-shell crabs and some other things . . ."

"What is a soft-shell crab?" asked Madame de Gaulle.

"All I know about them, Madame, is that you cut them as if they had never had a shell."

"Are they very good?"

"Neither better nor worse than an ordinary crab, but more picturesque. . . ."

"That was where you were able to talk seriously?" said the General. **"Curious!"**

"General, there at Robert Kennedy's house a handsome beige dog awaited the guests at the gates, and its brother, pitch black, waited at the entrance to the house. When I was to propose my toast, I said, 'Thank you for having us welcomed by a dog who appreciates that he must wear dinner clothes. . . .' General amusement. The United States isn't much given to protocol, and I have often had more serious discussions with Americans in this sort of cordial atmosphere than in what Europe would consider a serious setting.

"The President had just returned by air from a meeting at which he had expected two or three thousand people. There were three hundred thousand. He said to me, 'I am told the same thing happens in your country with General de Gaulle: why?' Because phonograph records have set the public clamoring for musicians, despite the prediction that their audiences would be destroyed. And you, General, your means of communication are more powerful than records. . . .

"Then at last we come to talk about France. I reminded him that we had been invaded many times, something that had never happened to the United States. And that in any discussion of the internal politics of France, it had to be understood that for us a government that did not provide for national defense could have only a *seeming* legitimacy. I take it you had told him that long before I did."

"Not exactly in that way. What did he answer?"

"More courteously than I sum it up, he said, 'We are Europe's defense.' To which in my turn I replied that national defense was the will to defend oneself, that he had seen this with Mao, and would find it out in Vietnam. He considered this; then he said, 'France is a curious country: its misfortunes following the victories that made it the first country of Europe, its rebuilt navy, the help she gave us, the Revolution, Napoleon, . . . 1940, and today General de Gaulle.' I told him it was a profoundly irrational country which found its soul (you recognize my pet theme) only in the course of finding it for others: with the Crusades, and with the Revolution, much more than with Napoleon. I said that Britain was at her greatest when she was left to herself, and that the Battle of Britain in 1940 had not been equaled since Drake—while France was great only when she was great for the world as a whole. . . ."

"There is a pact twenty centuries old between the grandeur of France and the liberty of others," said the General.

"I was well aware of what the President was thinking: the United States cannot base its European policy on France, but it cannot disregard France, because the French are always capable of inventing something unexpected: they have even invented General de Gaulle! . . . Kennedy went on to talk about the United States, and I said what I have said before to you—and had occasion to say also to the Minister for Foreign Affairs in Peking: 'The United States is the only nation to become the most powerful in the world without having sought their position by military means. Alexander wanted to be master of the world (his world, at least); so did Caesar. At times, the United States sought economic domination, but that is radically different. But now that it has this colossal power, we must see what it is going to do with it.'

"I had the impression that I had hit on his own thinking. Instinctively, he wanted the problems of Europe and of Asia to be decided by the United States; and that is why he had irritated me at our first meeting. I believe in the power of the United States, but I believe that power is one thing, and history is another. Carthage was powerful."

"Don't be deceived: he wanted at all costs to maintain the dominant position of the United States in the defense of the West. And despite his quality, I'm not sure that he did not accept the analogy so dear to the naive between a United States of Europe and the United States of America. But the latter was created from scratch, in a fertile Siberia, by successive waves of uprooted colonizers. If the United States becomes consciously master of the world, you'll see to what lengths its imperialism will go."

"Then I remembered President Eisenhower's anguished remark, 'I will not present myself before God with blood on my hands.' "

"Blood dries quickly."

"I said to Kennedy, with seeming casualness, 'You are now forced into a world policy, at least the way Rome was forced into a Mediterranean policy. Since the Marshall Plan, what has been the world policy of the United States?' And I had the feeling that he really wanted to take the burden of history on himself, to carry the enormous responsibility of the United States, which he was strongly aware of. Undoubtedly he would have done it. . . .

"I think it was by your declaration to him that he did,

in fact, bear that burden which set up the close relationship nothing destroyed. When his country was at issue, this very able politician was distinct from other politicians by his sudden bursts of anger. You remember his saying on television, 'My father always told me that when it comes to the country, businessmen behave like sons of bitches!' It may be that danger was already present; but from all the evidence, he had decided to disregard it. . . ."

"You know very well," replied the General, **"that courage always involves disregarding danger. And then, it is best to die assassinated or struck by lightning."**

He shrugged his shoulders. **"When Caesar was killed, he was holding the list of the conspirators in his hand, and had not read it. That poor President talked of Lincoln in a way that struck me. He was hoping to follow his path in life; and he followed it in death. And perhaps the somewhat obliging inattention of an obscure police chief in Dallas was enough to change the history of the world."**

"I believe the President died on your birthday. Destiny plays its mysterious game on its own: Shakespeare was born the year Michelangelo died, and the sun sets in the center of the Arc de Triomphe on the anniversary of the death of Napoleon, and he never saw it. . . . Louis XVI's last official act was to commission a lieutenant of artillery named Buonaparte. . . .

"Then, after some talk about history, the President said abruptly, 'China will have the atomic bomb soon. Should we intervene now?' My opinion was not important to him, but he thought I would answer differently from his American advisors, that I would bring him another kind of consideration. And he certainly expected that my answer would echo what you were thinking."

"If I remember correctly, you told him it would be a year before China had the atomic bomb?"

"Which was eventually the case. But what I did not understand, what I still did not understand later on when I was talking to the Chinese is this: why conceive of an American intervention in terms of a war—the Americans would certainly not land troops in China—instead of in terms of the destruction of a few Chinese industrial centers in order to set China back fifty years? I suppose he was asking me the question the Pentagon had put to him. I did answer that he had more time than he believed; and I added (very carefully . . .) that I thought he would not intervene."

The General fell silent. Was he wondering again what he would have done if he had had America's power and the atomic bomb available to him? Was he thinking of Russia? The snow was falling, as it falls on the Forbidden City.

"Kennedy certainly wanted some historic course of action, both for himself and for the United States. But it was no small thing to conceive a course for the world's most powerful nation, without its being an imperialistic operation. . . ."

"I have told you what I thought about it."

He made the gesture by which he seemed to want to chase everything away, and life first of all.

"Did you have an opportunity to see their great hippie gatherings?"

"I think most of them occurred in California. . . ."

"What do they really want?"

"A way of life. . . . Their ideology, like that of the groups before and after them, doesn't seem to me to be essential: the earlier rebels came from existentialism, the hippies from Gandhi, and the revolutionaries from Che Guevara. . . ."

"Guevara is more a character from your novels than from theirs. You know how he died?"

"I know what the Russians told me, and that must be what you mean. That he was in the hills with his Russo-Argentinian mistress, a Russian agent who, they say, handed him over?"

"But that was untrue."

"But that was untrue. She kept suggesting that he ought to organize the mine workers and give them control over the villages, which had been pretty well infiltrated by American agencies. But he had his memories of Cuba, and his Maoist illusions. . . . Thanks to this woman, and only thanks to her, the Russian agencies were able to protect him for several months. Then during a maquis engagement she took five bullets in the stomach. She died, and eleven days later he was handed over. . . ."

"That is almost exactly what I was told. You used to say about the young that the fundamental problem was authority. But it isn't the only one."

"There is nihilism. The girl at Nanterre who declared, 'When you know what you want, you have already become middle-class,' was quite revealing. The characters in *The Possessed* would have talked like her."

"What would she set against 'knowing what you want'?"

"Instinct. The events of May were born of the union between a revolt by the Communists—labor unionist, cautious—and an irrational revolt by youth. With links to the romantic sensibility, as it is everywhere."

"Not in Russia."

"Since the Kronstadt meeting, the sense of romantic anarchism has vanished from the Soviet Union. . . ."

"The Russian nihilists used to kill."

"And the Czar used to kill them. Seriousness has diminished a great deal. . . . Besides, the Russians were chaste, and they didn't take drugs. In this current phenomenon, there is a whole physical element. It is a compensation.

Revolution for the nihilists was a really supreme value which they connected with through action, as you've just said. The revolution our nihilists dream about is part of what I have called the lyrical illusion. What they would set up instead of the consumer society, which is uncertain to say the least in our country, is not another form of society; it is their indignation. But indignation is not a supreme value. A boy of twenty who carried out an investigation among the students told me, 'There is something bigger than the hippies and the revolutionaries: it is the number of young people who only say, "What does it matter?" ' Ambition has always existed, but the nineteenth-century middle class and its heir, the United States, made it the central passion. We may be witnessing an immense ebbing of ambition. Scarcely ten per cent of the students are politically minded. . . ."

"More of that complacent apathy! Indignation, indifference, brotherhood. . . . Poor Auriol used to say, 'I want to be President of a brotherly republic.' In order to become the master, the politician offers himself as servant. All over the world, we are going back to the day of men of good will, with nothing but the best. The day has gone by; destiny too. In 1914 I knew a young generation caught up by the curiosity that precedes first battles, and yet they felt the reaper coming. That generation is dead.

"The United States believed passionately that democracy would solve everything, and there it is, faced by a problem democracy won't solve. Their democracy is equality; it is also a feeling that places the Anglo-Saxon and Scandinavian democracies above ours: a worship of the Law. And when all is said, the Law is the State. In politics, in religion, the Latins have never been quite sure when they were Rome, and when they were pretending to be. Was it you who said that Rome was the opposite of Mediterranean restlessness?"

III In the drawing room with its leather armchairs, where we went to take coffee, Grigri was lying on one of them. The clouds had gathered, and the room was growing dark. With a touch of irony, the General said to me, **"It was you who invented the word Gaullism, wasn't it? What did you mean by it, in the beginning?"**

His tone had changed again. No more question of the casual familiarity with which he had spoken of Guevara, and even of Napoleon. As at intimate luncheons at the Élysée, the intermission was over.

I answered, "During the Resistance, something like political passions turned to serving France, as France used to serve the passions of the Right or the Left. Afterward, a feeling. For the majority of those who followed you, it does not seem to me that your ideology was the major element. The important thing was something else: during the war, obviously, it was the national will; afterward, and especially since 1958, it was the feeling that your motives, good or bad, *were not the motives of the politicians."*

"When I saw the politicians gathered together again for

the first time, I felt at once, no mistaking it, their hostility to everyone. They did not believe in the slightest that I was a dictator, but they understood I represented the State. That was just as bad: the State is the devil, and if it exists, then they do not. They lose what they value most, and that is not money but the exercise of their vanity. They all loathe the State."

"You didn't make life easy for them: they were promising gifts, you were promising sacrifices. But the fact remains that the French are anti-monarchist, and the organization of primary education since the Third Republic hasn't gone for nothing. They also are against politicians, often for bad reasons because, whatever may be said, I have seldom seen any corruption. . . . Guy Mollet told me he had less than eight hundred thousand old francs.* And it was certainly true. That reminds me: when his ministry and mine were opposite the Matignon, I had the old hall of the musketeers, which was flattering, and he had the old hall of the canons. . . ."

"I know big politicians are more honest than they are often said to be, but admit they are very fond of the national palaces. When Herriot came to see me, we hadn't talked five minutes before he was explaining why he should get back the Hotel de Lassay—the house attached to the Chamber. I didn't agree, because he wasn't president of the Assembly. He never forgave me."

"It seems to me that to earn the long-term esteem of the French a politician must be dedicated to some thing: France, peace—Clemenceau, Briand; even Poincaré, on account of the war. Those who stand for something more than a mixture of ambition and administrative ability. Those who are not merely politicians. You remember the crowd that stood up when I answered some miserable

*Head of the French government 1956–1957; held various offices up to 1959. Mollet's "fortune" would have been less than $1,600.

fellow who was attacking you, 'This is the man who, when our country was sunk in a terrible sleep, maintained its honor like an invincible dream!' And not everyone there was on our side."

"Yes. It will be the same when I am dead, you'll see. Why?"

"You gave the French a gift they hardly ever receive: the chance to choose their own better part. To justify sacrifice is perhaps the greatest thing a man can do. The Communists did that too, for their own people. Not for the others."

"Still, it was better to be Salan before our tribunals than Tukhachevsky*—who was innocent!—before Stalin's! But I recognize that if a great many soldiers in the year II died for the Republic, not one died for the radical party. And that France will go political again!"

"Your France has never been in the realm of the rational. Nor was the France of the Crusades, or of the year II. Why did the good men from the Isle of Sein come to join you? Why did we follow you? You used to say that in the end we might win; we thought that we would more probably be dead. The Gaullists on the Left really did hope that in the way of social reform, sooner or later you would do the things they no longer expected from the Communists or the Socialists; but that isn't why they followed you. In 1940, social justice was out of this world, Stalin was Hitler's ally, and Hitler was in Paris. The Communists joined us later, and were relieved to do so: the struggle for the downtrodden proletariat was at one with the struggle for defeated France."

"And for Russia."

"Gaullism was prevented from becoming a form of nationalism by its weakness. Your strength sprang from

*Russian general tried in secret for high treason and shot in 1937.

the fact that you had nothing. It was not only the Gaullists who followed you. To judge from the journalists who come to interview me, one major aspect of Fighting France and of the Resistance is on the point of disappearing, has already virtually disappeared: that is, anti-fascism. You are the last anti-fascist leader of the West. Most of the veterans of the Spanish Civil War, whether Spanish or French, who followed you after the Nazi-Soviet pact were continuing their own struggle. And were dumbfounded not to find Franco alongside Hitler and Mussolini."

"I'm glad to see you citing the foreigners, for what you are describing is the political Resistance, not the national Resistance; and without the second, the first would have had very little weight!"

"But they continued the struggle with us, rather than join up with the American army. And that too means something. I don't believe a future historian will be able to interpret Gaullism in purely political or even in purely national terms. Communism stands for the proletariat, but also for a will to justice that is not merely Marxist. Gaullism has been France, but something more as well. When one of my English friends arrived in Calais in 1945, he went into a bar, and above the counter was a large photograph of you. 'You're a Gaullist?' he asked the proprietor. 'Oh, you know, I don't go in for politics! But, after all, a man doesn't last much more than thirty years, and that guy's worth more than the rest. . . .' By chance, I was a passenger in the first private cruise made by 'La Marseillaise,' about 1950. The ministers of the Fourth Republic had just had a cruise in her. I ordered a particular wine. Then I realized that the wine steward would have to go miles to fetch it, and I changed my order. The wine steward smiled sadly. 'You changed your order to spare me from going down into the hold, didn't you? But I'm going. I'm happy to serve you. For our country, a great writer, that's fine. Not for them.' One reason, General, that people look on me as a sort of symbolic Gaullist is that I never ran for election. When you thought me too unserious in 1958, you suggested half in earnest, **'Be a minister!'** and I asked 'What for?' There are things in Gaullism that are self-explanatory, and some that are not. The most fitting description that has been used in homage to you is Soustelle's, *toward and against everything.* You were alone on the eighteenth of June, and you are alone today. Perhaps it had to be so. . . ."

"Whenever I was right, I had everyone against me."

"You say that the soldiers of the year II would not have died for the radical party, but our dead in the extermination camps would not have died for the election of the President of the Republic by universal suffrage—and I take the highest example."

What intrigued him in me was my mania for logic. There was no common measure between his epic role and my role; but while he had the genius of instinct, he also had a taste for rigorous thought. I remember his surprise when, on the question of devaluation, I told the Council his own thinking. He always spoke last. "I should like to understand," I said, "why Gaullism, which can only be the defense of the country against speculators—as it has been against so many other things—should accept devaluation when the experts insist that we can avoid it. . . ." And I expressed his more troubled sentiments when I said, "The destiny of France can stand a war in Algeria only if it ends in a settlement." And again, in May 1968, "Going to the Champs Élysées will commit us dangerously, unless there are enough of us. But perhaps there will be a million of us, and we ought to try." He did not need my remarks to reach that opinion, but he was pleased to hear me say it.

He looked at the card table. He obviously didn't believe in the cards. Why did they amuse him?

"We have kept a record of wins and losses for several months," said Madame de Gaulle. "The proportion is always the same."

The General raised his eyes. In his gaze, as in his voice, there was that weighty slowness I knew well.

"And later on, what will become of all that . . . ?"

Telepathy again. "Later" meant "when I am dead." Was he wondering what would happen to France, or to himself? At one moment he would think, **"Perhaps it is all ended"**; at another, **"France will yet astonish the world."** He had once said to me, with less pride than obsession, **"If a new burst of energy should occur, it will continue what I have done, and not whatever is done after me."** Was he thinking now of his eventual destiny? (His life no longer interested him.) Would he be considered an image of the French will? After all, Clemenceau had been that. In the library I noticed the tricolor binding of *Grandeur et misère d'une victoire.* I asked him, "What do you think now of Clemenceau?"

He answered vaguely, **"He despised people too much. But he believed in destiny. You remember the exchange: 'Franchet d'Esperey* was lucky!' said Lloyd George. 'That's a great deal already—so many people are not!' I am not sure that *baraka* exists: but the opposite certainly does.**

"Clemenceau's fury was an expression of France. It was in 1918—do you realize in 1918—that he replied with the famous interruption that is seen today as his first speech as president of the Council: 'In foreign policy, I am at war; in home policy, I am at war; Russia's betraying us, I am at war. I will fight before Paris, in Paris, behind Paris. And that's enough.' That was right. He knew the French. Think

*Louis Franchet d'Esperey (1856-1942), a French commander in World War I, made a Marshal of France 1921.

of the landscape that stretched before you this morning. It is an impregnable position. Vercingetorix lost it. Day after day Clemenceau had to receive union leaders and demonstrators."

"Clemenceau did make serious efforts to solve the problem. . . ."

"With what result? A tiger hunt?"

"Zaharoff,* who gave him his Rolls, used to take on as associates only people his cats liked. The shrewd ones put valerian on their trouser cuffs. Perhaps it is easier to fool cats than to fool history. . . . What do you think, Grigri?"

"It's astonishing that Clemenceau could have been a politician for so long, and suddenly stop. History transforms men. From time to time anyway. But he held onto his rages. He died hating Foch, with whom he had settled accounts; and Poincaré, with whom he hadn't. Philippe Berthelot, whom he had supported strongly against Poincaré, told him one day, 'You really are too harsh, Mr. President!' His answer was, 'I had a wife: she cuckolded me. Children—they have forsaken me. Friends—they have betrayed me. I still have these diseased hands, and I never take my gloves off. But I still have jaws too: I bite.' Berthelot added, 'It made me think of General Durakin: he was always angry, but no one knew why.' Very Parisian remark. . . . But Clemenceau had dared to tell the deputies, 'Drive me from the rostrum if what you are asking is not for the good of France, for I will not do it!' And to President Coolidge he said, 'Come to our villages and read the endless list of our dead, for comparison!' And, to whoever it might be, 'I would simply like the French people to dare to rely on themselves, and it is precisely that

*Sir Basil Zaharoff (1849-1936), an Anglo-Greek financier. For his large contributions to the cost of Allied propaganda and other services to the Allies, he was knighted in 1919.

spectacle that is denied me. The French have been sublime, and they didn't know it; they have become mediocre, and they don't believe it.' "

The wind has risen, and was making the snow spin around as it had spun in the garden of La Lanterne as I wrote the sayings of the clairvoyant who had discovered a bloody spot on an ancient cloth, without knowing that it was Alexander's blood.

"Themistocles," I said, "died in the service of Persia."

"Claude Monet used to quote a rather proud phrase of Clemenceau's: 'All honor to those who do not lower their eyes in the presence of destiny!' "

"Did you know Poincaré, General?"

"I was at the Gare de l'Est in 1914 when he came to see off the first troop trains. No one cheered, but all the civilians took off their hats. Death passing. There was something noble about it."

I imagined Captain de Gaulle in that courtyard at the Gare de l'Est where I had an appointment for that evening. And I thought of the Lancers I had seen milling in the dark in the Ardennes the day after the declaration of war in 1914.

Will the future agree with the proprietor of that bar in Calais? Stalin restored Peter the Great, and it was our republicans, beginning with Michelet, who restored Joan of Arc. Rational analyses are fragile. The radio? Was it enough to describe things correctly over the radio, to make Roosevelt despite his hostility—and even Hitler—understand that the corpse of France could be revived? What could the radio have done for General Giraud? How could he have said, "France is prostrate; but she is aware, she feels, she is still alive with a strong, deep tide of life. . . ." How to define Gandhi's historical action by his political action? How much did the history embodied by the General bear the accent of destiny? What would have happened if, after the Bordeaux interview, Herriot had agreed to take refuge in London? If Noguès had accepted the command of Free France, if Vichy had not outlawed freemasonry, and so caused half of French Africa to swing to the Gaullists? If Pétain had flown to Algiers? If Hitler had had the atomic bomb (which obsessed him) before the Americans? General de Gaulle's political skill had not ruled his destiny. The destiny of Saint-Just, of Joan of Arc, of Frederick II (the miracle of Brandenburg . . .), of Mao, had always disturbed me as the destiny of charmed figures. Two men could have barred Bonaparte's way: Saint-Just was guillotined, Hoche was poisoned.

At Le Petit-Clamart, it had been a near thing. The General regretted it, I believe.

In 1958, I was in charge of his safety for a time. We knew that someone was supposed to shoot at him from one of the marshals' houses around the Place de l'Étoile while he was standing at attention for the "Marseillaise" before the Arc de Triomphe. When I went into the office of Georges Pompidou, then head of the Cabinet, he was saying to a white-haired questioner, "Few kings of France have been assassinated: Henry III, Henry IV, . . ." "Yes, but they were the ones who tried to bring the French together . . . ," answered the questioner softly as he left the room.

"Who is that?" I asked.

"The prefect of police."

"Whatever may happen, General, if it should come from our adversaries—any of them from the sensitive souls at the Deux-Magots to your political enemies—God will be very much surprised. . . ."

"What adversaries? The Communists, who go from the Place de la Bastille to the Place de la Nation? The Social-

ists, who go nowhere at all? The labor unions, as if they could remake France? All that and Ferdinand Lopi.* It comes to the same thing, because it's all the same lack of power. Proud—of what?—of Mao Tse-tung's strength or Guevara's heroism? The Long March to end up at Charléty Stadium?† It's just not serious."

"And comedy besides. At the time of the referendum, my principal assistant, a Free Frenchman, said suavely to one of our leaders who was an anti-Gaullist, 'Unfortunately, if Malraux goes, we shall have to blacken the monuments again!' 'Oh,' was the answer, 'we'll make a plan: that will give us time!' Innumerable letters of insult reached my office because we had wasted the taxpayer's money on changing the color of Paris, destroying the precious patina of centuries—whereas in fact the stone of Paris, like that of Versailles, takes on an orange patina, never a black one. Anthology of fools. Anyway, they didn't replace you with Monsieur Poher.‡ As for your successors . . ."

"I have no successors, as you very well know. The Communists no longer have a sufficient belief in Communism, nor the others in the Revolution. It is too late. By force of their lying demands for democracy, they have become democrats! They want to threaten those in power; they no longer want to seize power.

"I don't see why an economic system called communism shouldn't be better than another called capitalism. I don't like 'isms.' But after all capital is plain enough, and so is free enterprise. I understand the American who says that

*An eccentric who proposed himself for the Presidency of the Republic but failed to secure a single vote on any occasion (he himself not being eligible to vote in Presidential elections).

†On May 27, 1968, 35,000 students and workers marched to demand De Gaulle to resign.

‡Alain Poher (1909-   ), became provisional President upon De Gaulle's sudden resignation in April 1969, then lost the election to Pompidou.

the postal services ought to be made private companies, like the telephone. I understand less well how free enterprise would provide Social Security. The answer will be that it ought to be able to do without it. Agreed. But if it had to set up an atomic bomb—which it might have been unable to create—against the bombs of the Soviet State, even the Chinese State—I wouldn't count on free enterprise. Enough of such childishness. I don't see why I should not have talked with the Communists as long as they were part of France and didn't create a sort of island within her, you understand. When I said to Thorez, 'You have made a choice. I understand you, but you have made a choice. I haven't the right to choose,' he did not agree, obviously, but he understood me too. The idea of the class struggle is a powerful one. I don't deny that. But it is contrary to all that is deepest within me. I don't want to set groups against one another, even to win out. *I want to bring them together.* At the time of the Liberation, I did that. That's why I shall never be a monarchist, whatever the agitators say. There is no possibility of uniting France around the Royal family. Nor is it possible to unite it around the working class, which is in the process of growing exhausted. Even the Communists had the word 'concrete' on their lips all the time, and they—the French Communists—are the most romantic party in the world. Very proud of a propaganda which has taught them that people who are convinced of everything in the lump can be convinced of everything in detail. They forget only one thing: none of that matters. *L'Humanité* says I joined Thorez in the Resistance. Stealing myths is useless, because a myth loses its power when it is separated from what gave it birth.

"In our country, it is impossible to base anything durable on a lie. That is a disturbing yet absolute fact. But in spite of appearances, Russian Communism is less of an impostor than any because the resurrection of Russia itself is not a lie."

"And because the social problem does exist."

"Perhaps Communism is in the process of becoming what political parties always do become: a myth in the service of a mutual aid society. Let's get ourselves some tires from the city government, in the name of the people's poverty. The future is not them, nor us, nor anyone else. We had to do what we did; but the future is that which doesn't yet exist. Like Christianity for the Roman philosophers.

"You know, the French have always found it difficult to work out a balance between their desire for privilege and their taste for equality. But in all this lot, my only enemy, and France's, has always been money.

"I had the intellectuals with me, but they turned into acrobats, as they were when they used to make epigrams on Rossbach in honor of Frederick II. Talent rarely guarantees correctness of ideas. And the radio strike, in May! Who went on strike for France in that organization when times were serious!"

"There are other intellectuals besides the customers at the Deux-Magots and the subscribers to *L'Observateur.*"

"Even they had been with me. You wrote that 'sensitive souls' were neither born nor died in 1788, and that historical romanticism is the present made history. Our sensitive souls called me a Maurras when I re-established the Republic, a colonialist when I created the Community, an imperialist when I went to Algeria to make peace there. Can you see Maurras going into battle to enforce universal suffrage in the Presidential elections? Can you see the Right delighted with the nationalization of industries, with my decisions on Algeria, with our Social Security system? In 1958 you know very well we were 'fascists.' You remember a phrase attributed to you, 'Has anyone ever seen a dictatorship coming up for a second ballot?' "

"I also said, 'Has anyone ever seen a dictator whom the press never stops attacking?' If the historians were to write your history from press reports, it would be astonishing."

On September 4, in the Place de la République, I introduced the speech in which the General outlined his Constitution. Hostile shouts from a distance grew faint in the huge square as the General was saying, "Then, in the midst of national anguish and foreign war, the Republic appeared! It was the sovereignty of the people, the call of liberty, the hope of justice. It was to remain that throughout the turbulent vicissitudes of its history. Today, more than ever, we want it to continue." That was the moment when the children's balloons floated nonchalantly up into the summer afternoon, their streamers crying fascism.

"The great French writers of the eighteenth century were prophets," he went on, "but what began as tragedy is ending once again in comedy. A pity! First because intellectuals, even when they delight in honors and puerilities, are, like me, serving something more important than themselves."

Camus, at the time of the crossing of the desert, asked as he left De Gaulle in what way he felt a writer could serve France. "Every man who writes" (a hesitation) "and writes well, serves France."

"All the same, there are some Gaullist artists," said I. "Braque and Le Corbusier yesterday, Chagall and Balthus today. And they are not alone."

"What is a Gaullist artist?"

"An artist who defends you."

"All right. You are as familiar as anyone with the complaint: we set France too high. As if they weren't aware how much cowardice there is in modesty!

"However, our intellectuals and our artists still count

for something in the world. I saw on television the funeral ceremonies you organized for Le Corbusier: the Cour Carrée of the Louvre, white again, lit up by floodlights, the ambassadors of Greece and India with their offerings. . . . The telegram the Indian government sent me: 'India, where stands the capital laid out by Le Corbusier, will come to pour on his ashes the water of the Ganges, in supreme homage.' The end of your funeral oration: 'Farewell, my old master and my old friend. . . .' Do you still remember how it went?"

> Farewell, my old master and my old friend. Good night. Here is homage from epic cities, wreaths from New York and from Brasília. Here is the sacred water of the Ganges and earth from the Acropolis. . . .

"Our sensitive souls would thrust off this heritage (moderately, it is true, in the case of Corbu, who made the academics sick), but they all have their Fathers of the Church, though they are hard to reconcile: Freud, Marx, Proust, Kafka, and so on. Patrology of enemies whose reconciliation will become incomprehensible when people have forgotten that the only life of the café schools was rationalizing irreconcilables."

"Desnos,"* he answered, **"and—what was that poor lad called?—Desbordes?—died nobly. Why don't the intellectuals believe in France any longer?"**

"Have they ever believed much in her? In the Middle Ages, France did not exist, but it was the subject of melancholy songs. Joan of Arc? Fifty years after her death, what was left of what she stood for? And Voltaire put an end to that. They believed in the King, or hated the King. For a man as intelligent as Diderot, liberty was Catherine

*Robert Desnos (1900-1945), a poet deported by the Germans to the concentration camp at Terezin in Czechoslovakia where he died.

of Russia! Negative passions play a very great part among the intellectuals; in our time, those who were against Hitler believed they were with you. At least, for a while. Add the mythology of the Left. Our intellectuals are nearly all of them literary people whose ideology depends on feelings. Why should a novelist understand policy or history better than a painter, better than a musician? Nietzsche wrote that since 1860 nihilism (which for him was what I have called the absurd) had little by little overtaken all artists. Since then, consider! Eighty per cent of genius, from Baudelaire to our present writers, has been nihilists. Without this conversion, the problem of the young would be different. And this conversion is extraordinarily profound."

"There's no doubt about that. The absurd, as you call it, can work against the nation. I was not born to defend it. Yes, the conflict was deferred by anti-fascism and by the Resistance. But our intellectuals want what they call the spirit, as little spiritual as it is, to rule the nation. (To end up with May '68!) As for myself, I want liberty of the spirit to be defended at all costs, except at the cost of the national reality on which it is built. Voltaire, whatever he may have thought, was more closely linked with France than with Reason. The intellectuals get enthusiastic over intentions, and we over results. What is to be done about it? Give luncheons?

"Pompidou thought people should always be brought to lunch together. Was he wrong? I invited Adenauer, whom I hardly knew. People who detested one another because they didn't know one another—you give them lunch off the same leg of mutton, and that turns them into sheep."

He turned to look at the falling snow. He belonged not to our times—but to a millennial past which his massive stature suited, now, like a recumbent figure on a tomb.

"Before a century has gone by, what we call the Right

and the Left will have joined the chimeras, and will be scarcely intelligible. As it should be. Understand that I am suspicious of political theories not on principle, but from experience. When the Popular Front came into power, I thought: since they must fight fascism first of all, they will be obliged to defend France. Therefore, they would have to build a modern army. I knew poor Lagrange, the only member of parliament who went to fight—he died of it. I knew Blum slightly. What happened? The Popular Front built the French army of 1918—of 1918!—when the Nazis were building the armored divisions I had asked for, and their *Stukas!* "

"The Popular Front did a great deal else."

"Which without me would have been swept away by Hitler and by Vichy. The Russian government fought on the main point. Hitler too. Since ancient Greece, the Mediterranean has accepted speeches as reforms. All that we did. . . . People want to forget that it was we who did it. As you know very well, when the Common Market was created it would have been fatal to us, burdened as we were by our agriculture, if we had joined the Six without guarantees. But France continues to be devastated by myths.

"And I too am a myth. In a different way.

"Modern historians delude themselves that a man in power can do what he wants to do. Louis XIV complained that he was powerless in Auvergne, where the people accused in the Poisons case took refuge with the governor. Napoleon complained he had no control at Orléans (at Orléans!) unless he went there. And I was unable to get suitable buildings put up in Les Halles. But I wanted to revive France and, to a certain extent, I did so. As for the details, God will recognize his own. He will explain, poor thing, why the Leftists call themselves Leftists to distinguish themselves from the Communists, and have as-

sumed that description only since the Left ceased to exist."

"There is a very active historical romanticism in this Left, the hand-on-heart element of Victor Hugo's old men who come forward to speak their truths to Kings. In Mediterranean countries, politics is linked with theater. The romantic element has sometimes worked for you, sometimes against you."

"You are right. As I said, they were for me as long as they saw me as Tintin. They adore Tintin."

"But, if the Left was for a long time something other than a comedy, that was because it opposed the Right, which was primarily money."

"The Right ceased to have an ideology when it ceased to ally itself with the nation; and when the heritage of Rome which it shared with the army, the Church, and the State was taken over by the Communists—who were (obviously) not the Church, who infiltrated the army, and who aimed to become the State."

"A Right based on profit can be only a clandestine Right. The old myth of the Left was the same as the myth of Gaullism in 1940: the defense of the defeated. That myth has justified in turn the National Convention, the revolutionaries of 1848, the Communards, the shrewder Radicals, the Bolsheviks, the Left Wingers of May. . . . A political myth is a body of emotions which moves into ideas as the hermit crab moves into the shells of dead mollusks. . . ."

"The Commune wanted to take on France, and for that reason it is part of French history. But it never killed a single Prussian."

"The intellectuals look on the Commune favorably, on the Revolution of 1848 unfavorably. But rabid idyllism dates from long before 1848: Rousseau knew it, so did Saint-Just. Historical romanticism has become one of the fundamental elements of our civilization."

"If you throw it out, what remains of the revolutionary myth in Marxism?"

"Collective ownership of the means of production, don't you think? But our Marxists seem to be in no doubt about it. For a long time, the electoral Left has relied on anti-clericalism, especially in its connection with freemasonry. . . . That is coming to an end. I can easily imagine a serious Marxist replying to the Left Wing lyrical illusion, 'General de Gaulle's power is the son of his action during the war—the son, not the brother!—and would have been inconceivable without the development of the third sector.' Consider that this year, in France, that sector has overtaken the other two, peasants and workers, combined. But the objective of our sensitive souls is not to seize power: it's to seize the Odéon Theater."*

"Yes. At the time of the Liberation, the political fauna took me for an amateur. And though I was well acquainted with them, I was disconcerted by their incapacity to know what they were talking about. Revolution? I was the only revolutionary. There were the Communists, of course: for them the word meant seizure of power by their party. And years later, in May 1968, their leader said to our Minister of the Interior, 'Don't give way!' But the others! "

"Is there any important word that doesn't draw its power from superimposed meanings?—Revolution, God, love, history. . . . God means creator, judge, sacred love, the mystery of the world. Beyond that . . ."

"There is no need to define God; but there is to define what people want to change, and the means by which they want to change it. All the same, there do exist—I can't deny it—great obscure epochs of history. I once tried to discover what really divided the Blues from the Greens at Byzantium.† In vain. Whereas I understand Rome."

*The National Theater in Paris, occupied by students May 15-June 14, 1968.
†Political factions in Byzantium in the sixth century.

"I believe the metamorphosis of myths is as little predictable as the metamorphosis of works of art. At Leningrad, I saw the Czarina's room: its walls were dotted with portraits of Rasputin. I have watched the parade of absurdities accepted by so many of our intelligent contemporaries with the same astonishment that, later on, I read accounts of the Moscow trials. Perhaps as a matter of fact we can comprehend Rome—at least up to Tiberius. . . . And the October Revolution. The acceptance of guilt by the Moscow defendants is a different matter. And so is the allegation that the CRS,* who killed no one, were murderers; that there had to be a march, in May, with great banners saying, 'Let us avenge our dead!' when there were no dead; that the GPU, and in another area my friend Mao, represent liberty. After he had represented for others, and just as understandably, the man with a knife between his teeth. . . . I wish I could understand the wizards of my own period."

"The history of chimeras has yet to be written."

"Although the destruction of capitalism has never been fundamental for you. . . ."

"I didn't come to destroy capitalism. But on the other hand, I didn't defend it. I came to re-establish France as against the myths that were destroying her reality. Did Lenin know he had come to re-establish Russia?

"Perhaps politics is the art of putting fantasies in their place? People do nothing serious if they give in to chimeras—but how to do anything great without them?"

"In certain respects, France too is a chimera. . . ."

"No. Chimeras are what does not exist. Marxism is not a chimera. Nor Lenin. Nor Stalin. Nor Mussolini either. The chimera is the Marxism of the intellectuals who have not read Marx. Your sensitive souls have undoubtedly

**Compagnies Républicaines de Sécurité:* mobile police units under civil authority.

read many things by Jean-Jacques Rousseau, but not *Le Contrat social*—which, despite its reputation, is a powerful book."

"It isn't only in the political domain that fantasies hold sway."

"Have you met the parish priest of Colombey? He's a good priest. He said to me about extreme unction, 'I have nearly always found the same attitude, especially among women: Vicar, I'll do as you say, but, you know, it's not terribly important. I have never done harm to anyone; the good Lord won't refuse me.' I realize it would be interesting to determine exactly what Catholics do believe. Men hardly know when they are dying; still, this priest is right. There are more Christians who believe that God will welcome those who have never done evil than there are Christians who believe in hell. We are too ready to accept the idea that men believe in their banners. Each of us had his little personal faith in his own little bag, believe me—Marxists as well as Catholics. . . . But it isn't quite the same thing: to each his own Republic. The chimeras of the spirit remind me rather of fashions."

"I have never decided exactly what I think of fashions. Feminine fashion is a means of social acceptance: admitted. But the centuries when men must wear beards, the centuries when they must be clean-shaven. . . . In the realm of religion, the problem is equally mysterious. The sensitive souls, bound to the political comedy, obviously become play-actors—or suicides, The women the Colombey priest was describing are not play-actors."

I thought about his own faith, which I had never grasped. The Church was a part of his life, but he said to the Pope, "**And now, Holy Father, suppose we speak of France?**" He very rarely mentioned God, and not at all in his last will and testament. He never mentioned Christ. I was accustomed to his silence on certain major topics, a silence born of an invulnerable sense of decency and of great pride—if the feeling, "this concerns me alone," can be called pride. He took communion at Moscow for obvious reasons: he was bearing witness. But he took communion not only at Moscow. I believe his faith was so deep that it ignored every domain that would put it in question. That is why my agnosticism did not bother him. (And because I am neither anti-clerical nor anti-Christian, at a time when so many intellectuals are, whereas those of his youth—Péguy, Jammes Claudel—were not. He was intrigued rather than annoyed by an agnostic friendly to Christianity, even one who was also friendly to Hinduism.) His faith was not a question: it was a given, like France. But he liked to speak of his France; he did not like to speak of his religion. A God, supreme judge, who inspired him to pardon the condemned, or helped him divine the fate of France? That faith covered a secret realm which was probably that of Christ, and also a questioning—not into faith, but into the forms it takes. He had been struck when I quoted him the Hindu saying, "Each man moves toward God through his own gods." He asked me one day, **"What do you see as the meaning of religious works by such colossi as Beethoven and Victor Hugo, whose Christian faith was dim but who were, nonetheless, not Voltaireans?"**

At all events, this faith has been nurtured by two thousand years. Deep and mysterious. One day, one of his closest aides whom he had asked to do the research he would need for his next speech (in Canada, I think?) said to him timidly, "I thought you might want to end with something about divine will, and the material is there."

He answered, **"Thank you. I am not afraid of God."**

Of course, his words meant, "Did you think I would be ashamed to refer to God?" But Freud would not have taken lightly the form he chose. . . .

I said, "At the end of his life Gide set great store by an idea which has always struck me as extraordinary: 'For me, religion is an extension of morality.' He had obviously once thought the reverse. . . ."

"Sin is not interesting. The only ethic is one that leads man toward the highest he has within himself. The highest may not be very high, but that doesn't matter! Religion can no more be an extension of morality than morality can be a dependency of religion. None of that is serious. Man is not made to be guilty. The serious thing is to understand why dead passions—political, moral, and so on—are dead. And to defend what manages to survive, in mysterious ways. But do not forget that André Gide was a writer for whom history raised no questions because, in his eyes, it did not exist.

"How strange it is! Valéry spoke very ill of history, but he wrote several incomparable interpretations of it: it was a family quarrel. I'm pleased I gave him a State funeral. At the end of his life, history was what men *do*. He abstractedly watched it die."

How many passions we have seen of which nothing more will remain than *L'Action française* does for the students at Nanterre! They had forgotten even its name. Nothing more than of the political passions that have battled in this world of mine, as religious passions battled through so many centuries. . . . Who among my readers under thirty, among my readers abroad, remembers that *L'Action française* ruled the Sorbonne? In a hundred years' time, who will be able to tolerate the vocabulary without laughing—alienation, structure, demystification, Malthusian forces, progressivism, consumer civilization . . . ?

He continued rather musingly, **"When I said, 'I have come to deliver France from the fantasies that hinder her from being France,' I was understood. But they are too** constant, they play too important a role, to permit us to think they merely buzz around history like flies. They succeed one another too. Have they a history? Queer creatures! They range from puerile Mediterranean indignation to serious realms; from the Left Bank's Leftism to the sentiment of your sensitive souls who in another time found themselves facing the guillotine. Yesterday, when I was out walking, the shadow of the clouds was passing at my feet; and it occurred to me that fantasies belong to humanity in the same way that the clouds belong to the sky. But do fantasies succeed one another like clouds, or like plants? At the sight of the large trees that stand to the right of the gate, I often think of the history of nations. It is the reverse of the clouds. All the same, to take France on oneself, in 1940, was no gardener's problem!

"So, I watch the fantasies pass by. I come indoors. I pick up these books again. They have survived and have perhaps shaped men, as successive gardeners have shaped my trees. After all, the word culture means something. What endures—what does not? You understand. . . . I'm talking about a deeper opposition than between the ephemeral and the lasting, you understand; of what is mysterious in the fact of duration. This library is not a collection of truths as opposed to nonsense. Something else is involved."

"What are you re-reading?"

"Aeschylus, Shakespeare, the *Mémoires d'outre-tombe,* a little Claudel. And what people send me, which generally belongs with the clouds. I answer everyone who sends me a book: they might easily not send them."

"Do you still like Rostand?"

"His youthfulness is endearing. But I do not reflect on my youth, nor even on Claudel. I reflect on the major works of other times—in some degree of other civilizations. I can only explain myself by an image. Those writers

I re-read—add Sophocles to them—. . ."

"Another general."

". . . give me the sense of stars all lighted by the same invisible sun. They have something in common. Like the trees, although . . . they are different from clouds and from chimeras: they have something permanent to them. A kind of transcendency? So I walk between the clouds and the trees in the same way as between the dreams of men and their history. Then there comes a feeling that intrigues me. Those great poems—I have very little liking for the theater, but at present I am re-reading only dramatic poems—I know very well they meant something different for their time than they do for us: I have written you in the past my thoughts on your theory of metamorphosis. But what are they for history? You were saying a while ago that this word is one of those whose depth comes from their manifold meanings. That is certainly true. But we must understand what we did."

"What *you* did."

"What I did was never defined for me by what I was doing. Particularly not the eighteenth of June. The important thing—perhaps the most important thing for all men who have been involved with history—was not what I said, but the hope I roused. So far as the world goes, if I have renewed France, it is because I renewed hope in France. Could anyone be obsessed by a vocation without hope, I ask you? When I am dead, that hope will cease to mean anything, because its strength depended on our future which, obviously, will no longer be a future. Then what you call metamorphosis will occur. Not that I fear none of this hope will remain. A Constitution is an envelope: what is inside it can be changed. While what was inside counted, who the devil would throw it into the wastebasket? But the fate of what counted is unpredictable. A man of history is a leaven, a seed. A chestnut tree does not resemble a chestnut. If what I did had not carried hope within it, how could I have done it? Action and hope are inseparable. It certainly seems that only human beings are capable of hope. And remember that in the individual the end of hope is the beginning of death."

"Time and again, you have, in fact, been the symbol of hope."

"Perhaps you were right to say that for a great many people, what defined Gaullism was what separated them from the politicians. But for me, when I accepted the word —rather late—it was the energy of our country, the rediscovered energy. That is why the first volume of my memoirs will be called *Mémoires d'espoir.* And that is why I am preparing the second volume (don't let's talk about the third!) with very different feelings. What we did is about to be transformed, and I want a testimony to exist: 'Here is what I wanted. This, and no other thing.' That is why the only ministers I have now are the clouds, the trees, and, in a different way, books."

"You know the saying, 'The quivering of a branch against the sky is more important than Hitler'?"

"And than cancer, no doubt—when it is neither your own nor that of a being you love! Oddly feminine saying."

"A man said it, I believe."

"I suppose Hitler used to say it to those who preferred to defend themselves with branches rather than with tanks. But, after all, I understand its intended meaning. For some months, I have observed a great many branches."

"One could desire to be in harmony with the life that is not the life of men."

"I like trees. I also like woodcutters. And then, in the saying you quoted, I fear the word 'important' could simply mean 'lasting.' The branch was not more important than Hitler for our comrades in the extermination camps! The course of history is not merely the behavior of a single man, even when that man is Napoleon. It takes on the deepest passions, or the distress, of many men, and shares them. How could one not see the trees, here? After all, France has lasted longer than the oldest branch in the park. Don't let us be dupes of eternity. Of the short eternity of branches. . . . There is no need of eternity to understand the limits of action—misfortune is enough."

Was he thinking of his walks with Anne?

"You know the exchange between the eighty-year old Moltke and Bismarck?"

"Which one, General?"

" 'After such events,' said Bismarck, 'is there anything left worth experiencing?'—'Yes, Your Excellency,' answered Moltke, 'watching a tree grow.' "

"Even from the metaphysical or religious point of view, to free prisoners from an extermination camp is not less 'important' than the existence of trees, even of spiral nebulae. Unfortunately, history consists of more than setting people free. . . ."

Dostoevsky contrasted the branch with Evil, and that morning I had said that sacrifice or heroism did not appear to me less profound than Evil. But it seemed to me that over the last twenty years, for the General, history had been a domain all of whose servants were alike. In my view, there are two types of men of history, and they have in common only the fact of their survival. On the one hand are the conquerors; on the other the liberators and those who are somehow connected with them. We are moved by Philopoemen and Vercingetorix probably because we see them as defeated liberators.

"History certainly does not consist only of setting people free," he said. "It is confrontation. Of the enemy, of destiny too. Perhaps greatness is founded only on the level of confrontation."

He had always thought in these terms. And his thought

had not changed, even in confronting the life of the trees or the drift of the clouds. I too, often. But he was rooted in France, like his trees. For him, history was action: the shadows of the clouds follow upon one another in continuous course over this ancient earth whose eternity he contemplated. For me, history was mainly their irregular sequence, the Heraclitean flow of the river. And yet, like him, I could not come to terms with the branch. Rather than a lesson, it seemed to me an accusation. . . . He went on, "Perhaps we have not been aware enough of an obvious, but noteworthy fact: men of history are necessarily gamblers."

When he spoke in a confidential tone, he screwed up his eyes, and the confidence seemed ironical. "Saint Bernard could not be sure he would crush Abelard. Napoleon, on the morning of Austerlitz, could not be sure of victory. At Borodino, he thought he was the victor because the Russians had abandoned the field. 'How many prisoners?' 'Sire, scarcely any.' Only then did he understand that he had joined an unreal battle, and gained an unreal victory. Even Alexander the Great must have wondered, before his encounter with Poros, how his Indian campaign would turn out. The uncertainty of great politics is not so very different from military uncertainty.

"No historian has attempted to analyze the most curious element in history: the moment at which *the current begins to flow*. For us or against us: the Wehrmacht in 1940 and 1944; the Liberation and May 1968. It does not flow by chance, I am sure. Still, what makes it flow is never decisive. Sometimes it disappears as rapidly as it has come. I'm not referring to what makes a man of history suddenly abandon history, as did so many Romans, the Emperor Charles V, and your friend Saint-Just. I'm speaking of what gives a soul to a people—or to an army."

I thought of Algeria, and especially of Vietnam. How

often in the past I had heard, "You'll never make an army out of the Annamese!" I replied, "The mysterious current exists in art as well. Baudelaire, Picasso. . . ."

"And *Cyrano.* Perhaps it is what Rome called Fortune. We are continually being reminded that real history is not defined by a series of battles. True enough. But then they assert that it is defined instead by the invention of the yoke and harness (a view set forth by Commandant Lefebvre-Desnouettes—another military man!), by the class struggle, or by the rise and fall of cultures. I realize that we cannot define history by the procession of what we do not know. Nonetheless! In all Napoleon wrote, I am most intrigued by the events that surprised him, disconcerted him. . . .

"Well, in a few days it will be 1970. . . . Only one generation separates the West from the appearance of the Third World on the stage. In the United States, it is already in position."

"It is the end of the age of empires."

"Not only of empires. Gandhi, Churchill, Stalin, Nehru, even Kennedy. It is the funeral procession of a world."

He raised his arms in the gesture he had made familiar to us, though I had never see him make it before except in public.

I thought of the funeral pyre and the glowing bullets that fell from Gandhi's corpse; of the whistles of Russian trains announcing the death of Stalin across the Siberian wastes; of Churchill's escort and Kennedy's; of Nehru's elephants. My life.

"There still remain Mao and, to some degree, Nasser," I said.

"Mao, yes. Islam, perhaps. Africa—who knows?"

I was thinking not of Africa, but of the Asia of my youth. The Asia of the past, an Asia without a present, that had toppled in the night. Innumerable little balloons carrying luminous advertisements among the stars of Osaka; the endless files of the Chinese people past the Forbidden City; the multitudes around Gandhi, with the flowers falling from the trees as he began to speak. . . . A billion humans, almost unchanged for a thousand years, and manacled to their past by Europe. Now, the impatient rumbling that was also the obsequies of a world. And soon—Africa? I thought of my airplane in 1959 in the dawn above the vast swamps of the Chad; of the black soldier who fainted under the moderate sun of the Place de la Concorde that July fourteenth when the flags of the Community were being distributed. . . . And of President Senghor, of the "negritude" he proclaimed while the Merovingian queen of the Casamance,* with her great cat, led her faithful followers under the sparkling cascade of kapok toward the sacred trees. Senghor too proclaimed the arrival of the Third World. . . . Last plunge into Asia, thousands of gladioli bent in a single gesture, Mao, the Forbidden City, the great sun of China through the curtains of white silk. . . . In 2000 will the Third World be confronting the civilization that conquered the moon and lost its youth, in which students set themselves aflame like Buddhist priests? All who were in this room now would be dead. . . . Without noticing what he was doing, the General scattered the playing cards on the green table and watched the falling of the Australian snow.

"They'll set up a great cross of Lorraine on the highest hill there. It will be visible to everyone, but as there is no one, no one will see it. It will rouse the rabbits to resistance."

In the direction of the hill there was nothing, as far as the eye could see, but the undulations of the Merovingian forest.

*An experience in Africa described in *Antimémoires*.

"Stalin was right: in the end death is the only winner."

"Perhaps," I said, "the important thing is that it doesn't win immediately . . . ? Perhaps it's the same problem as the one you raised in relation to the library, and which comes up in relation to the museum too. . . . Compared to the spiral nebulae, the Soviet Union, France, the two thousand five hundred years Aeschylus has endured . . . why does man passionately want to win the first battle against death? Egypt believed that after thousands of years mummies, statues, pyramids would no longer protect the Pharaoh. But she built the pyramids."

"There was nothing else to be done. . . ."

He was seventy-eight or seventy-nine years old. **"I don't pretend that age was not a factor in my decision,"** he had said. He seemed to me now much older than I was; we only notice the aging of others. His authority remained startling, and his dialogue was not with old age, but with a "what does it matter?" stoicism which sometimes questioned the history he himself had made. Death had no importance, but had life much more? In the solitude of Colombey, he was certainly writing those *Mémoires* on the margin of a rambling colloquy with death. And yet . . . ? In a speech he made in 1940, he quoted, "Man of the plain, why do you climb the mountain?" "The better to see the plain." In the past, when I had mentioned religious feeling, he would answer me with that gesture of his like brushing flies away.

"Some fools who for the most part have done nothing themselves," he said, "have complained of 'my inconsistencies.' As though the world in which I had to act hadn't changed! As if a consistent policy was always the same! They must suppose that living consists in imitating childhood, wanting jam at any price!"

"I don't believe the world has ever before changed so much in one generation, even at the fall of Rome. . . ."

before hippies and revolutionaries, but the teachers then didn't turn into rebels. Valéry said to me about Gide, 'I can't take seriously a man who worries over the judgment of young people.' I answered that youth and young people are not the same thing."

"To be sure: like France and the French. But has there been a civilization before ours in which the great old men were enemies of their youth? You said the teachers of the Middle Ages didn't become rebels. You see, there is something that cannot go on: the irresponsibility of intellect. Either that will stop or Western civilization will stop. Intellect could be concerned with the soul, with the cosmos, as it was for so long, simply with life, with itself—whatever. It has concerned itself with temporal life, with politics, in the broad sense. The more it is concerned with politics, the more irresponsible it becomes. In Russia, in China, it doesn't do so. Montesquieu would have told me something important. But when I have questioned our intellectuals, they have said things that were simply inconsequential. You understand? They were playing a role. Often disinterestedly, sometimes with generosity. With generosity, but without consequence. Now, stupidity can talk and say nothing; intelligence cannot. You will see. The intellectuals must rediscover what they think. It is possible to fight for unclear passions; it is not possible—you understand?—always to fight for nonsense. The end result is the selling of Left Wing newspapers on the streets: not for lack of courage, not at all, but because this courage never confronts its enemy. If I had told Stalin that before long, in our country, the declared enemies of the State (of the government, if you like) wouldn't manage to get arrested, he would have thought I had gone mad."

"How did you begin when you met Stalin?"

"For at least a minute, no one spoke. It seemed a long time. Then . . ." He shrugged his shoulders. "Then, I

expected him to speak of Europe, or of his people at Lublin—he was so devoted to them! But he said, 'So you are going to ask me to hand Thorez over?' He went on, 'In your place, I shouldn't have him shot: he is a good Frenchman.' I answered, 'The French government treats Frenchmen in the light of what it expects of them. And you?' "

The General hardly ever told anecdotes. **"Stalin stories —Churchill liked that kind of thing."** But others took his place. I had heard about the banquet at the Kremlin, when an imprudent Russian minister proposed a toast to Stalin, a thing which was simply not done. Stalin lifted the glass containing his own vodka, which was water—he never drank alcohol except in his own apartments—and said, "Comrade So-and-So is Minister of Transport, and if transport doesn't keep moving . . ." (Stalin smashed his glass on the table) "he will be *hanged.*" It was this he had in mind when the General said to me, **"He was an Asiatic despot, and that was what he wanted to be."**

As for the Lublin government, the General refused to recognize it. The banquet ended, and he went up to bed. At three o'clock in the morning, Molotov, having failed to find Bidault, the Minister of Foreign Affairs, came to Gaston Palewski and said, "Will you tell General de Gaulle that the marshal is going to show a film for him?" The General went down to the small hall in the Kremlin. It was a patriotic film, with German soldiers falling one after the other in close-up. At each death, Stalin's hand contracted on the General's thigh. **"When I judged he had made me sufficiently black-and-blue, I drew my leg away."**

Hitler was still alive. . . . In the morning, the Franco-Soviet pact was signed. The snow was undoubtedly like the snow that surrounded us now—thicker. . . .

When Serge Eisenstein was ordered to stop the production of *La Condition humaine,* he confided to me, "I was left in peace when I was making *Potemkin* because I was almost unknown, because they gave me six weeks to make the film, and because if it turned out badly, so much the worse for me. I was twenty-seven. But I won't ask Stalin for an audience now because, if he doesn't understand, all I can do is kill myself."

He had described to me, in 1934, a similar scene with Chaplin, when he had shown him photographs of Chinese beheadings; Shakespeare made minor characters replay the greatest scenes in his masterpieces; so does God. And how did Eisenstein die?

"Here's the only interesting thing I have been told about Stalin," said the General. **"He thought he was alone, but Molotov was behind him. With his two hands he covered large parts of the world globe that stood in his study; then, with one hand, Europe, and murmured, 'It's small, Europe. . . .'**

"But I met Stalin, I did not meet Russia. My Poland: that was a different story. I'm sorry, it's Russia that counts!"

"You would have seen in the life of the Soviet Union that marvelous extravagance so many great Russian writers have conjured up—it continues to exist. Stalin used to quote, 'Among us, there is Sparta and Byzantium. When it is Sparta, all's well." Byzantium is not the only opposition to Sparta; there are the inspired drunkards, Soviet comedy which is no gayer than Russian comedy, and a realm difficult to define.

"In 1934, I knew the chief of police for the Far North. The natives were getting alcohol—which was killing them. Something had to be done about it. After some weeks of dog sledging, my GPU chief reached a sort of isle on the Arctic Ocean. He found bottles of vodka, a dead Russian preserved by the cold, some penguins or other animals, and, on what served as a table, a page from a San Francisco newspaper, with a marriage advertisement surrounded by a black line drawn with a half-burnt stick: 'Young lady, respectable and of good family, would like to marry a Russian, preferably Siberian, of similar standing.' Date of the newspaper: 1883. Several bundles of roubles beside it, held down by a stone.

"And the Rostov Club, almost all of whose members had lost a limb, because the club's purpose was to paste the cathedral domes over with signs made of notebook pages (there was no paper): they said 'God is a traitor.' Why didn't they go to prison (they ended up there, I expect, but I was in Rostov before the purges), since God was a traitor because he had delivered Russia up to the Bolsheviks? A mystery. But God kept things going: each year some of the sign stickers would fall and break a leg or an arm—and the cripples would take their vodka with their pals who were going to break a limb next year.

" 'Russia is still full of Karamazovs,' Ehrenburg used to say. I was with him when I came across my best Russian story. In some Siberian town, posters hang in the factories with Stalin's signature: 'Sexual relations are henceforth forbidden.' Constant speeches: 'Comrades, all that time spent on individual satisfactions is lost to production! Sexual indulgence is worse than vodka!' 'Then,' said Ehrenburg, 'I go to post office, I ask for telegram. Post office girl, blond braids, twenty years old, says: "Comrade Ehrenburg, I tore it up. It said, 'Sexual relations between men are forbidden.' Idiots in Moscow! As if there could be sexual relations between men!" So, very not pleased, I said, "Comrade post office girl, you, idiot! *Dourak!*" '

"There are endless numbers of such anecdotes. And I don't believe they have no significance."

"No."

"As in Russian novels, they touch on something profound. Last year I saw a Komsomol who was overwhelmed at reading an exercise book in which the Gospel according to Saint John had been copied out, a handwritten exercise book that cost as much as the complete works of Tolstoy. I listened to a psychiatrist (today in Moscow it is possible to speak: the hand of the police is still over people's heads, very close to them, but it no longer holds them by the throat) who told me, 'I have just been treating the son of a people's commissar. I asked the traditional question: "What is your most frequent dream?" "That I am alone at last. Apart from everyone else. Alone against the world. . . ."' Once long ago, Bukharin and I were pacing the Place de L'Odéon—it was surrounded with sewer pipes taken up out of their trenches—and in a distracted tone he confided, 'And now he is going to kill me.'

"And he did.

"I think a great deal about the Poles, probably because General Anders' adjutant is a friend of mine. When we consider Poland and Russia, we are considering a relationship almost as distant as the relationship between China and Korea. . . . When the Soviet Union entered the war (if that is the way to put it!), the Polish prisoners in Russia were lined up in military formation to listen to a Polish officer who was to tell them they would be joining the Polish army of liberation, fighting alongside the Red army. The officer moved forward slowly, leaning on two canes, because a month earlier he had been tortured by the Russians. . . .

"You remember Stalin looking hilarious for the photographers at the signing of the German-Soviet pact? Obviously, he had seen it all before. Djilas, who met him at about the same time you did, said he was bald. Ten years earlier, he had been a hardy police officer, silently interested in the world, the terror, his pipe, and his straight mustache. . . ."

"When I met him, he had become an old, all-powerful cat. Bald? That might have gone with Byzantium. He was a cat prowling at the edge of a funeral pyre; a wildcat. He claimed his alliance was with the future, and what impressed me most was his rootedness in the past."

"The past is always there, in Russia! In Lenin's office beside maps of the civil war fronts, a small bronze Darwinian apeman stood on a pile of Marx's works. It had been given him by a United States industrialist who wanted to build pencil factories now that the Soviet government had decided to teach children to write. Culture, you know! I saw the play made out of *Ten Days that Shook the World*. It was thrilling, but pure myth—much more than Eisenstein's inspired *October*. Next day I visited the Marx-Engels museum. It was empty enough for me to find several pairs of lovers clasped together in the last room, more secluded than on the benches in the square. . . . And then of course, the colossal resurrection of Leningrad, the graveyard with five hundred thousand dead, the uninspired but epic monument at Stalingrad,* which is indeed a monument out of Sparta. . . ."

"And beyond the picturesque?"

"I met Stalin at Gorki's house: cunning and strange. Quiet joviality. Later, the real thing. I believe he was activated by statistical passion—as profoundly as you are by the will to bring people together: if we kill all the people who knew the people who knew, and so on, we will get at the real criminals, or we will paralyze them. 'While I am in charge there will never be a Franco.' The innocence of the people he killed or sent to prison was of no interest to him. Do you remember his answer to Djilas's protests over the Red army's rapes in Yugoslavia? 'They have gone through so much they shouldn't be

*Renamed Volgograd in 1961.

called to account!' And above all what clarified him for me, far more even than the trials: Russians who had been taken prisoner were all sent to jail, even those who had escaped."

"Statistical obsession does not explain the despot. He is drawn to it."

"You remember his conversation with Bukharin while he was still in the government: 'To settle the problem of the Kulaks according to your theory,' Bukharin said, 'we would have to start by killing eight million of them.' 'Well . . . ?' He had an odd kind of geniality, rather fascinating; in short, a serpent in mustache.

"Then there was my last talk with Kosygin. Of course he was a politician, nonetheless he *was* the sole survivor of the three directors of the Plan—Stalin had killed the other two. And he *had* nonetheless been mayor of Leningrad during the siege, and I was not quick to forget the largest civilian graveyard in the world. But the talk was the same as with Chou En-lai: that mixture, so disconcerting to us, of masterful historic views, and then assertions that seem to assume the interviewer is a half-wit. Kosygin talked to me about Mao's culpable personal power, and about the progress of humanity: 'Men cannot be stitched into a uniform pair of trousers, or you risk turning out nothing more than soldiers! The time of the fanatics is over.' And then, 'There is as much difference between the Party you knew and the Party today as between the Moscow you knew and that city today.' Indeed! Incidentally, I think that is true. But not that the Party has ceased to be the Party. Obsessed by Mao, by his will to conquer Asia. But also by the speculation, 'What is his support? The intelligentsia is against him. He is the dictatorship, and it will lead to capitalism. When he dies, there will be a vacuum. Everything he does is based on fear.' 'Fear is a great power, Mr. President.' Suddenly, he grew serious:

'The Chinese may eventually intervene in Vietnam. . . .' (Where, as we all know, the Soviet Union never intervenes!) 'They are for war, whereas we are for peace.' 'In your opinion, Mr. President, will the United States make use of the atomic bomb?' 'No.' 'The Chinese speak continually of war, but they don't wage it. Even in Vietnam. I am not sure that the forces for peace can make peace, but I am sure that the forces for war cannot make war, at least for the time being. . . .'

"The snow was falling as it is here, but in large flakes, and before that window which had been Stalin's, I was thinking of the speech I had made on the permanence of nations: 'Stalin, watching from the window of the Kremlin the falling of the snow that had shrouded the Teutonic Knights and Napoleon's *Grande Armée*. . . .'

"In 1934, when I left him, I thought, in the little square below the Kremlin, of this immense, miserable country, menaced by Hitler and already desperate to rival the colossus America. I looked up at the medieval towers above me, and thought of the Imperial Guard of skyscrapers in Manhattan, and of the Siberian steppes where, like the beginning of a conflagration, the lights of great industrial plants blazed in what was still wilderness.

"But my last Russian memory has nothing to do with Stalin or his successors. A friend of mine, an émigré of 1918, asked me to go and see his mother in Moscow, and to help her. Which I did. Some months after my return we were watching a film, and he suddenly said to me, 'My mother looks like that old woman on the screen, now, doesn't she?' "

The snow-tired car which was to take us back to Bar had just entered the courtyard. The General walked us out, and added, as if he did not want to end this modest but superlative hospitality without returning to the essential, "Remember what I told you: I mean there to be no common ground between me and what is happening now."

"Before ten years have gone by, you will have been transformed into a romantic character. There will still linger somewhere—a vague eighteenth of June, a vague decolonization."

"A vague France?"

"A vague France. Over against it will be the wise men. Then, among the surviving Gaullists, something unpredictable will happen. And among the young—oh, much later, of course!—something of the same kind. When Joinville wrote his *Vie de Saint Louis* he was old. Joan of Arc was right at Patay, another eighteenth of June, in the year 1429. And then? The reality you took in your grasp will not be your final heir: the chief figures of our history remain in every mind because they served something besides reality."

He answered, with a lassitude that had nothing to do with fatigue, "In politics, there is a strategy, which is probably called history. And then there is tactics: to speak of that is no more serious than to speak of swordsmanship. Everyone is familiar with Napoleon's dictum, 'War is a simple art; everything is in the execution.' It is wise to reflect before acting, but action is not born directly of reflection. It is something else. As I have said to you before, an historic destiny is sure to involve many mistakes. I was not too much mistaken about France, not about what had to be done for her. And yet I believed that Russia would never succeed in making the bomb; that in 1946 war was inevitable; that in 1947 France could not go on. In 1960, Adenauer told me that if the Socialists came to power in Bonn, they would treat with Moscow. We were mistaken. But I was not mistaken about the destiny of France. I was not mistaken when I asserted that Pétain would not go to Algiers. You were right to say, 'The road through Montoire* leads to Sigmaringen.'† One should never go by way of Montoire. But people can think, quite rightly, that France must at all costs oppose the reconstitution of a Reich, and still lay a wreath to the German unknown soldier. It is time that makes history. If France's history goes by way of independence for Algeria, let it! By way of our marriage with Germany, let it! Regretting Algerian independence was not pleasant. But the important thing was to know that we had the responsibility for France. Contrary to what politicians think, politicians do nothing. They gather territories together until they lose them, and they defend interests until they betray them. History is accomplished in other ways.

"Do you know what might well have been the reality?

"Those characters believe I left because of Monsieur Mitterrand, Monsieur . . . what's his name?—Poher. In fact, I left because of what you were describing a while ago. France was the soul of Christianity—today, let us say, the soul of European civilization. I did all I could to restore her. The month of May, politicians' games—not worth discussing. I tried to prepare France for the end of a certain kind of world. Did I fail? It will be for others to see later on. We are certainly witnessing the end of Europe. Why should parliamentary democracy (involving as it does here in France the distribution of tobacco outlets!), which is on its last legs everywhere, be capable of creating Europe? Good luck to this federation without a federator! But after all, they must be fools! Why assume that a type of democracy that nearly killed us, and which is unable to assure even the development of Belgium, is sacred when it comes to surmounting the enormous obsta-

*Montoire-sur-le-Loir, where Laval and Pétain met with Hitler and Ribbentrop in 1940 in an attempt to define the policy of Franco-German collaboration.

†German town, south of Stuttgart, where Pétain lived in a Hohenzollern castle after he left Vichy.

cles that confront the creation of Europe? I have never believed in trusting the fate of a country to some principle that vanishes when that country is threatened. And should I agree to entrust Europe to such a principle . . . ?

"They are obsessed by democracy now that it has ceased to exist. Anti-fascism has a broad back. What democracy? Stalin, Gomulka, Tito, yesterday Peron? Mao? The United States had its monarch—Roosevelt—and misses him. Kennedy's illusions are doomed. You know as well as I do that Europe will be a compact among the States, or nothing. Therefore, nothing. We are the last Europeans in Europe, which was Christianity. A tattered Europe, but it did exist. The Europe whose nations hated one another had more reality than the Europe of today. It is no longer a matter of wondering whether France will make Europe, it is a matter of understanding that she is threatened with death through the death of Europe.

"After all, what was Europe at the time of Alexander? These woods you have seen, the woods I see every day. . . ."

That morning they spread out behind him to infinity and took on an insidious presence when he made them a partner in the conversation.

"The fury of the students—episodes! Confessionals were set up to fend off the devil, and then the devil was put into the confessionals. True democracy is ahead of us, not behind us: it has still to be created. Of course, there is another question, one that dominates everything: in the first civilization without faith, the nation may gain time, Communism may believe it is gaining. I can accept that a civilization may be without faith, as you say, but I should like to know what it uses instead, consciously or unconsciously. To be sure, nothing is final. What would happen if France became France again? I learned that gathering the French together always remains to be done over again.

But perhaps this time the stake hardly concerns her. When all is said, I shall have done what I could. If we must watch Europe die, let us watch: it doesn't happen every day."

"Then the Atlantic civilization will arrive. . . ."

"France has seen others. As I said to you before it didn't look very bright the day of the treaty of Brétigny, nor even on the eighteenth of June. . . ."

We reached the entrance. The General gave us his hand, and looked at the first stars, in a great hole of sky, to the left of the clouds. He said, "They confirm the insignificance of things."

The car started. Still the white snow on the black trees. The upholding of France against all odds, the miserable Resistance, that whole desperate adventure—illusions! Decolonization, the end of the Algerian drama, the man who was the emblem of ravaged France speaking equal to equal with the President of the United States—illusions! I remembered a union worker in the riots of 1934: he carried a red and black flag,* and at the sight of the charging police, the leaders were shouting, "Put away the flags! Yes, yes—let's not rush things. . . ."

The light of the snow, centuries of half-light in which the Merovingian steeples stood; times when the church clocks watched over Christianity with the indifference of their single, serene hand. . . . Senghor's little clock striking in his air-conditioned office at Dakar, and the warm air trembling against the windows—is the weather good in Dakar? The leaders of the new African nations, who think of Europe only because of the help they can get from her, do they dream of a united Africa? A huge Black follows his donkey in a deserted alley. What does Africa matter to General de Gaulle, or Mao who had just reconquered China, or the passions which have swept over nations like

*Symbolizing Communism (red) and anarchism (black).

great birds of prey—what did even the nations matter? And what importance to Mao, to the queen of the Casamance, was the ephemeral swirl of this ancient snow, and its everlasting companions, the clouds above the surviving steeples and the vanished graveyards? I thought of the savages of Borneo, all wearing stopped wrist watches there in the bush. And probably because I feared obscurely that I had seen the General for the last time, I thought of Nehru's house—and of Benares.

> I am the death of everything, I am the birth of everything—word and memory, constancy and mercy—and the silence of secret things. . . .

The Ganges was carrying away blue and red gleams in the night,

> Pronounce now the useless words of wisdom. . . .

Dim lights in the dead-ends of Benares, and in the past at the end of the alleys of Ur or of Babylon, the sound of barking in the depths of the star-spangled night. At Provins, in 1940, our colonel was waiting for orders. As soldiers must never be left without occupation, the men who were to fight against armor, now at ease, were instructed to look for four-leaved clovers. . . . I thought of the moon glow which suddenly filled our armored car as we were charging the German lines . . . of the evening in June 1940, full of roses in the gunfire and the summer fog, when peasants were burning their ricks before the night. Of the chaplain who died at Glières. On a snowy night like the one coming on, we were advancing in Indian file. He was carrying the automatic rifle. I slowed down to wait for him, and asked him, "What are you thinking about?" "Nothing: I am trying to see Christ. . . ."